MENTAL HEALTH ATLAS 2014

WHO Library Cataloguing-in-Publication Data:

Mental health atlas 2014.

1.Mental Health Services - statistics. 2.Mental Health Services - atlases. 3.Health Policy - trends. 4.Health Personnel - statistics. 5.Global Health. I.World Health Organization.

ISBN 978 92 4 156501 1
(NLM classification: WM 17)

© World Health Organization 2015

All rights reserved. Publications of the World Health Organization are available on the WHO website (www.who.int) or can be purchased from WHO Press, World Health Organization, 20 Avenue Appia, 1211 Geneva 27, Switzerland (tel.: +41 22 791 3264; fax: +41 22 791 4857; e-mail: bookorders@who.int).

Requests for permission to reproduce or translate WHO publications –whether for sale or for non-commercial distribution– should be addressed to WHO Press through the WHO website (www.who.int/about/licensing/copyright_form/en/index.html).

The designations employed and the presentation of the material in this publication do not imply the expression of any opinion whatsoever on the part of the World Health Organization concerning the legal status of any country, territory, city or area or of its authorities, or concerning the delimitation of its frontiers or boundaries. Dotted and dashed lines on maps represent approximate border lines for which there may not yet be full agreement.

The mention of specific companies or of certain manufacturers' products does not imply that they are endorsed or recommended by the World Health Organization in preference to others of a similar nature that are not mentioned. Errors and omissions excepted, the names of proprietary products are distinguished by initial capital letters.

All reasonable precautions have been taken by the World Health Organization to verify the information contained in this publication. However, the published material is being distributed without warranty of any kind, either expressed or implied. The responsibility for the interpretation and use of the material lies with the reader. In no event shall the World Health Organization be liable for damages arising from its use.

Design: Erica Lefstad

Printed in France

CONTENTS

6	PROJECT TEAMS AND PARTNERS
7	PREFACE
8	EXECUTIVE SUMMARY
12	INTRODUCTION
16	RESULTS
18	1. GLOBAL REPORTING ON CORE MENTAL HEALTH INDICATORS
22	2. MENTAL HEALTH SYSTEM GOVERNANCE
30	3. FINANCIAL AND HUMAN RESOURCES FOR MENTAL HEALTH
38	4. MENTAL HEALTH SERVICE AVAILABILITY AND UPTAKE
46	5. MENTAL HEALTH PROMOTION AND PREVENTION
52	6. COMPARISONS WITH SELECTED MENTAL HEALTH ATLAS 2011 RESULTS
56	REFERENCES
58	APPENDICES
58	APPENDIX A: PARTICIPATING COUNTRIES AND CONTRIBUTORS MENTAL HEALTH SYSTEM GOVERNANCE
64	APPENDIX B: GLOSSARY OF TERMS

PROJECT TEAM AND PARTNERS

Atlas is a project of the World Health Organization (WHO) Headquarters, Geneva and is supervised and coordinated by Shekhar Saxena. Mental health Atlas 2014 is the latest in a series of publications that first appeared in 2001, with subsequent updates published in 2005 and 2011.

In WHO Member States, key project collaborators were the mental health focal points in Ministries of Health, who provided information and responses to the Atlas survey questionnaire and to follow-up queries for clarification. A full list of collaborators is provided as Appendix A of this report.

Key collaborators from WHO regional offices, who contributed to the planning and collation of data and liaised with focal points in Member States, were: Sebastiana Da Gama Nkomo (WHO Regional Office for Africa); Jorge Rodriguez, Devora Kestel (WHO Regional Office for the Americas); Khalid Saeed (WHO Regional Office for the Eastern Mediterranean); Matthijs Muijen and Elena Shevkun (WHO Regional Office for Europe); Nazneen Anwar (WHO Regional Office for South East Asia); Xiangdong Wang, Yutaro Setoya and Marie Villanueva (WHO Regional Office for the Western Pacific).

At WHO Headquarters, a team comprising Dan Chisholm, Fahmy Hanna and Grazia Motturi provided the central technical leadership and administrative support to the project, including development of the questionnaire and an associated completion guide, management of the online data collection system, validation of information and responses, liaison with Member States and WHO regional and country offices, as well as analysis of data and preparation of this report. They received inputs and advice from the following colleagues: Natalie Drew, Tarun Dua, Alexandra Fleischmann, Michelle Funk, Vladimir Poznyak, Chiara Servili, Mark van Ommeren and Taghi Yasamy. The contribution of Antonio Lora, Peter Ventevogel, Julian Eaton, Yulia Bakonina, Melissa Harper, Elise Gehring, Pooja Pradeep, Shelly Chopra and Alessandra Trianni to particular aspects of data collection, processing, or analysis are also acknowledged.

The development of the Atlas 2014 questionnaire was overseen and approved by an expert group, consisting of Florence Baingana, Harry Minas, Antonio Lora, Crick Lund, Pratap Sharan and Graham Thornicroft. The proposed set of selected indicators were subsequently field-tested in Chile, South Africa, Vietnam, and for this stage thanks go to Sifiso Phakathi, Melvyn Freeman, Alfredo Pemjean, Harry Minas and Ritsuko Kakuma.

The contribution of each of these team members and partners, which has been crucial to the success of this project, is very warmly acknowledged.

PREFACE

WHO's Mental Health Atlas series has already established itself as the single most comprehensive and most widely used source of global information on mental health situation. This new edition of Mental Health Atlas, carried out in 2014, assumes new importance as a repository of mental health information in WHO Member States because it is providing much of the baseline data against which progress towards the objectives and targets of the Comprehensive Mental Health Action Plan 2013-2020 is to be measured. The Action Plan contains four objectives:

(1) To strengthen effective leadership and governance for mental health

(2) To provide comprehensive, integrated and responsive mental health and social care services in community-based settings

(3) To implement strategies for promotion and prevention in mental health

(4) To strengthen information systems, evidence and research for mental health

Global targets have been established for each of these objectives to measure collective action and achievement by Member States towards the overall goal of the Action Plan. Atlas is the mechanism through which indicators in relation to agreed global targets, as well as a set of other core mental health indicators, are being collected. In collecting this information, the mental health Atlas 2014 questionnaire covers critical areas of mental health system development, including governance and financing, human resources, service availability and delivery, promotion and prevention, and surveillance.

Subsequent to this baseline data collection in 2014, a Mental Health Atlas survey will be sent to country focal points periodically, so that progress towards meeting the targets of the Action Plan can be measured over time.

Dr Shekhar Saxena

Director, Department of Mental Health and Substance Abuse, World Health Organization, Geneva, Switzerland

EXECUTIVE SUMMARY

WHO's mental health Atlas project dates back to 2000, when a first assessment of available mental health resources in WHO Member States was carried out (WHO, 2001). Subsequent updates have been published since then (WHO, 2005; WHO, 2011).

The 2014 version of mental health Atlas continues to provide up-to-date information on the availability of mental health services and resources across the world, including financial allocations, human resources and specialised facilities for mental health. This information was obtained via a questionnaire sent to designated focal points in each WHO Member State. Latest key findings are presented to the right.

KEY FINDINGS

GLOBAL REPORTING ON CORE MENTAL HEALTH INDICATORS

- 171 out of WHO's 194 Member States (88%) at least partially completed the Atlas questionnaire; the submission rate exceeded 80% in all WHO Regions;

- 60% of Member States were able to report on a set of five core indicators that covered mental health policy and law, promotion and prevention programmes, service availability and mental health workforce;

- 33% of Member States regularly compile mental health service activity data covering at least the public sector.

MENTAL HEALTH SYSTEM GOVERNANCE

- 68% of WHO Member States have a stand-alone policy or plan for mental health; 51% have a stand-alone mental health law. In many countries, however, policies and laws are not fully in line with human rights instruments, implementation is weak and persons with mental disorders and family members are only partially involved.

FINANCIAL AND HUMAN RESOURCES FOR MENTAL HEALTH

- Levels of public expenditures on mental health are very low in low and middle-income countries (less than US$ 2 per capita). A large proportion of these funds go to inpatient care, especially mental hospitals;

- Globally, the median number of mental health workers is 9 per 100,000 population, but there is extreme variation (from below 1 per 100,000 population in low-income countries to over 50 in high-income countries).

MENTAL HEALTH SERVICE AVAILABILITY AND UPTAKE

- The median number of mental health beds per 100,000 population ranges below five in low and lower-middle income countries to over 50 in high-income countries; equally large disparities exist for outpatient services and welfare support.

MENTAL HEALTH PROMOTION AND PREVENTION

- 41% of WHO Member States have at least two functioning mental health promotion and prevention programmes; out of more than 400 reported programmes, over half were aimed at improving mental health literacy or combating stigma.

EXECUTIVE SUMMARY

In a new development, Atlas is also being used to track progress in the implementation of WHO's Mental Health Action Plan 2013-2020. Specifically, mental health Atlas 2014 is providing baseline values for agreed Action Plan targets; further rounds of mental health Atlas will enable monitoring of progress towards meeting these targets by the year 2020.

Baseline values for the year 2013 are given in the Table to the right for each of the six Action Plan targets, based on Atlas 2014 findings. They show that the percentage of countries fulfilling the condition of these targets is already quite substantial, suggesting that the global targets can be successfully reached if progressive development is made in relation to mental health policies, laws, programmes and information systems across WHO Member States. However, Atlas 2014 does not provide sufficiently robust data to establish a baseline for the target on service coverage. Other data sources suggest that the current rate of service coverage for severe mental disorders remains low, which indicates that substantial additional effort will be needed to achieve target 2 on service coverage.

MENTAL HEALTH ACTION PLAN 2013-2030: BASELINE VALUES FOR GLOBAL TARGETS

Action Plan Objective	Action Plan Target	Baseline value for 2013
OBJECTIVE 1: To strengthen effective leadership and governance for mental health	**Target 1.1:** 80% of countries will have developed or updated their policies or plans for mental health in line with international and regional human rights instruments (by the year 2020).	88 countries, equivalent to 56% of those countries who responded, or 45% of all WHO Member States. Value is based on a self-rating checklist (see Section 2.1 of report).
	Target 1.2: 50% of countries will have developed or updated their law for mental health in line with international and regional human rights instruments (by the year 2020).	65 countries, equivalent to 42% of those countries who responded, or 34% of all WHO Member States. Value is based on a self-rating checklist (see Section 2.2 of report).
OBJECTIVE 2: To provide comprehensive, integrated and responsive mental health and social care services in community-based settings	**Target 2:** Service coverage for severe mental disorders will have increased by 20% (by the year 2020).	Not computable from Atlas 2014 data, but expected to be less than 25%, based on treatment gap and service uptake studies.
OBJECTIVE 3: To implement strategies for promotion and prevention in mental health	**Target 3.1:** 80% of countries will have at least two functioning national, multisectoral mental health promotion and prevention programmes (by the year 2020)	80 countries, equivalent to 48% of those countries who responded, or 41% of all WHO Member States. Value is based on a self-completed inventory of current programmes (see Section 4 of report).
	Target 3.2: The rate of suicide in countries will be reduced by 10% (by the year 2020).	11.4 per 100,000 population. Value is based on age-standardized global estimate (see WHO report on suicide, 2014).
OBJECTIVE 4: To strengthen information systems, evidence and research for mental health	**Target 4:** 80% of countries will be routinely collecting and reporting at least a core set of mental health indicators every two years through their national health and social information systems (by the year 2020).	64 countries, equivalent to 42% of those countries who responded, or 33% of all WHO Member States. Value is based on a self-rated ability to regularly compile mental health specific data that covers at least the public sector (see Section 1 of report).

INTRODUCTION

WHO first produced an Atlas of Mental Health Resources around the world in 2001, with updates produced in 2005 and 2011 (http://www.who.int/mental_health/evidence/atlasmnh). The Atlas project has become a valuable resource on global information on mental health and an important tool for developing and planning mental health services within countries.

2014 UPDATE

This new edition of Mental Health Atlas, carried out in 2014, assumes new importance as a repository of mental health information in WHO Member States because it is providing much of the baseline data against which progress towards the objectives and targets of the *Comprehensive Mental Health Action Plan 2013-2020* is to be measured. A total of six global targets have been established for the four objectives of the Action Plan to measure collective action and achievement by Member States towards the overall goal of the Action Plan (see the left-hand section of Table 1 to the right).

As stated in the Action Plan, the indicators underpinning the six global targets represent only a subset of the information and reporting needs that Member States require to be able to adequately monitor their own mental health policies and programmes. Thus it was agreed that the WHO Secretariat would prepare and propose a more complete set of indicators for Member States to consider and if approved, use this as the basis for data collection and reporting to WHO.

The final proposed set shown below represents the culmination of this consultation and field-testing process, and is made up of the already agreed Action Plan indicators (shown in green in the summary table) and a complementary set of Service development indicators (shown in blue). These fourteen indicators became the basis for the Mental Health Atlas questionnaire that was sent to all WHO Member States in mid-2014. Since most of the collated data that has been reported on by countries relates to activities or available resources in 2013, the results of this Mental Health Atlas survey constitute an appropriate baseline measurement for the *Comprehensive Mental Health Action Plan 2013-2020*.

Subsequent to this baseline data collection in 2014, a Mental Health Atlas survey will be sent to country focal points periodically, so that progress towards meeting the targets of the Action Plan can be measured over time.

TABLE 1: CORE MENTAL HEALTH INDICATORS, BY MENTAL HEALTH ACTION PLAN OBJECTIVE AND TARGET

Action Plan Objective	Action Plan Target	Action Plan Indicators	Service development indicators
OBJECTIVE 1: To strengthen effective leadership and governance for mental health	**Target 1.1:** 80% of countries will have developed or updated their policies or plans for mental health in line with international and regional human rights instruments (by the year 2020).	1.1. Existence of a national policy/plan for mental health that is in line with international and regional human rights instruments	**2a. Financial resources:** Government health expenditure on mental health **2b. Human resources:** Number of mental health workers **2c. Capacity building:** Number and proportion of primary care staff trained in mental health **2d. Stakeholder involvement:** Participation of associations of persons with mental disorders and family members in service planning and development **2e. Service availability:** Number of mental health care facilities at different levels of service delivery **2f. Inpatient care:** Number and proportion of admissions for severe mental disorders to inpatient mental health facilities that a) exceed one year and b) are involuntary **2g. Service continuity:** Number of persons with a severe mental disorder discharged from a mental or general hospital in the last year who were followed up within one month by community-based health services **2h. Social support:** Number of persons with a severe mental disorder who receive disability payments or income support
	Target 1.2: 50% of countries will have developed or updated their law for mental health in line with international and regional human rights instruments (by the year 2020).	1.2. Existence of a national law covering mental health that is in line with international and regional human rights instruments	
OBJECTIVE 2: To provide comprehensive, integrated and responsive mental health and social care services in community-based settings	**Target 2:** Service coverage for severe mental disorders will have increased by 20% (by the year 2020).	2. Number and proportion of persons with a severe mental disorder who received mental health care in the last year	
OBJECTIVE 3: To implement strategies for promotion and prevention in mental health	**Target 3.1:** 80% of countries will have at least two functioning national, multisectoral mental health promotion and prevention programmes (by the year 2020)	3.1. Functioning programmes of multisectoral mental health promotion and prevention in existence	
	Target 3.2: The rate of suicide in countries will be reduced by 10% (by the year 2020).	3.2. Number of suicide deaths per year	
OBJECTIVE 4: To strengthen information systems, evidence and research for mental health	**Target 4:** 80% of countries will be routinely collecting and reporting at least a core set of mental health indicators every two years through their national health and social information systems (by the year 2020).	4. Core set of mental health indicators routinely collected and reported every two years	

INTRODUCTION

METHODOLOGY

The Mental Health Atlas project required a number of administrative and methodological steps, starting from the development of the questionnaire and ending with the statistical analyses and presentation of data. The sequence of steps followed was in line with that pursued in 2011, and is briefly outlined below.

STAGE 1: QUESTIONNAIRE DEVELOPMENT AND TESTING

As described above, the selection of indicators to be included in the questionnaire was based on consultations with Member States, and developed in collaboration with WHO regional offices as well as experts in the area of mental health care measurement. A draft version of the questionnaire was piloted in two countries, and also sent to Regional Advisors for Mental Health as well as other experts for their feedback. The questionnaire was modified based on this feedback. The questionnaire was drafted in English and translated into three official United Nations languages – French, Russian and Spanish. The final version sent to countries for completion can be found at the mental health Atlas website (http://www.who.int/mental_health/evidence/atlasmnh). Alongside the questions, a completion guide was developed to help standardize terms and to ensure that the conceptualization or definition of resources were understood by all respondents. A glossary of terms was also developed and shared with respondents (see Appendix B).

STAGE 2: QUESTIONNAIRE DISSEMINATION AND SUBMISSION

In the respective countries, WHO headquarters together with WHO regional and country offices requested ministries of health or other responsible ministries to appoint a focal point to complete the Atlas questionnaire. The focal point was encouraged to contact other experts in the field to obtain information relevant to answering the survey questions.

Close contact with the focal points was maintained during the course of their nomination and through questionnaire submission. Staff members at WHO headquarters and regional offices were available to respond to enquiries, to provide additional guidance, and to assist focal points in filling out the Atlas questionnaire. The Atlas questionnaire was available on-line, and countries were strongly encouraged to use this method for submission. However, an off-line version of the questionnaire was available whenever preferred.

STAGE 3: DATA CLARIFICATION, CLEANING AND ANALYSIS

Once a completed questionnaire was received, it was screened for incomplete and inconsistent answers. To ensure high quality data, respondents were contacted again and were asked to respond to the requests for clarification and to correct their responses.

Upon receipt of the final questionnaires, data were aggregated, analysed and are reported both by WHO region and by World Bank income group. For some sections, for example those dealing with availability of human and financial resources, reporting by income group is more informative, while for others (such as governance) the primary reporting is by WHO region. As of 1 July 2014, low-income economies are defined as those with a gross national income (GNI) per capita of $1,045 or less in 2013; middle-income economies are those with a GNI per capita of more than $1,045 but less than $12,746; high-income economies are those with a GNI per capita of $12,746 or more. Lower-middle-income and upper-middle-income economies are separated at a GNI per capita of $4,125. Lists of countries by WHO region and by World Bank income group are provided at Appendix A. Frequency distributions and measures of central tendency were calculated as appropriate for these country groupings. Rates per 100,000 population were calculated for certain data points, using official UN population estimates for 2013.

LIMITATIONS

A number of limitations should be kept in mind when examining the results.

While best attempts have been made to obtain information from countries on all variables, some countries could not provide data for a number of indicators. The most common reason for the missing data is that such data simply do not exist within the countries. Also, in some cases it was difficult for countries to report the information in the manner specifically requested in the Atlas questionnaire. For example, some countries had difficulty providing information about the mental health budget in the requested format because mental health care in their country is integrated within the primary care system, or is broken down using different expenditure or disease categories. Also, in some countries, health budgets are devolved down to the sub-national level, which can greatly complicate the estimation of consolidated expenditures at a federal level. There were similar difficulties experienced in relation to the estimation of service use or uptake and also the extent of social care and welfare support for persons with severe or other mental disorders. The extent of missing data can be determined from the number of countries that have or have not been able to supply details. Each individual table or figure contains the number of countries able to respond to an item of the questionnaire, or the equivalent percent (out of a total of 194 WHO Member States).

A further limitation is that most of the information provided relates to the country as a whole, thereby overlooking potentially important variability within countries concerning, for example, the degree of policy implementation, the availability of services and the existence of promotion or prevention programmes in remote or rural areas versus urban areas. Similarly, few of the reported data can provide a breakdown by age or gender, despite the place that equality of access and universal health coverage has in the articulation of the Comprehensive Mental Health Action Plan 2013-2020. This makes it difficult to assess resources for particular populations within a country such as children, adolescents, or the elderly (although such information was secured in relation to mental health promotion and prevention programmes).

Finally, it is important to acknowledge the limitations associated with self-reported data, particularly in relation to qualitative assessments or judgements (often being made by a single focal point). For example, respondents were asked to provide an informed categorical response concerning the implementation of mental health policies and laws, and their conformity with international (or regional) human rights instruments. For some of these items it is possible to compare self-reported responses to publicly available information (such as a published mental health policy or budget for a country), but in other cases the opportunity for external validation is more limited.

Project Atlas is an on-going activity of the WHO. As more accurate and comprehensive information covering all aspects of mental health resources become available and the concepts and definitions of resources become more refined, it is expected that the database will also become better organized and more reliable. For example, an increasing number of countries are implementing the WHO System of Health Accounts 2011, which holds out the prospect of better estimation of government mental health expenditures. While it is clear that, in many cases, countries' information systems are weak, it is hoped that the Atlas may serve as a catalyst for further development by demonstrating the utility of such information for national planning, monitoring and evaluation.

RESULTS

RESULTS

1. GLOBAL REPORTING ON CORE MENTAL HEALTH INDICATORS

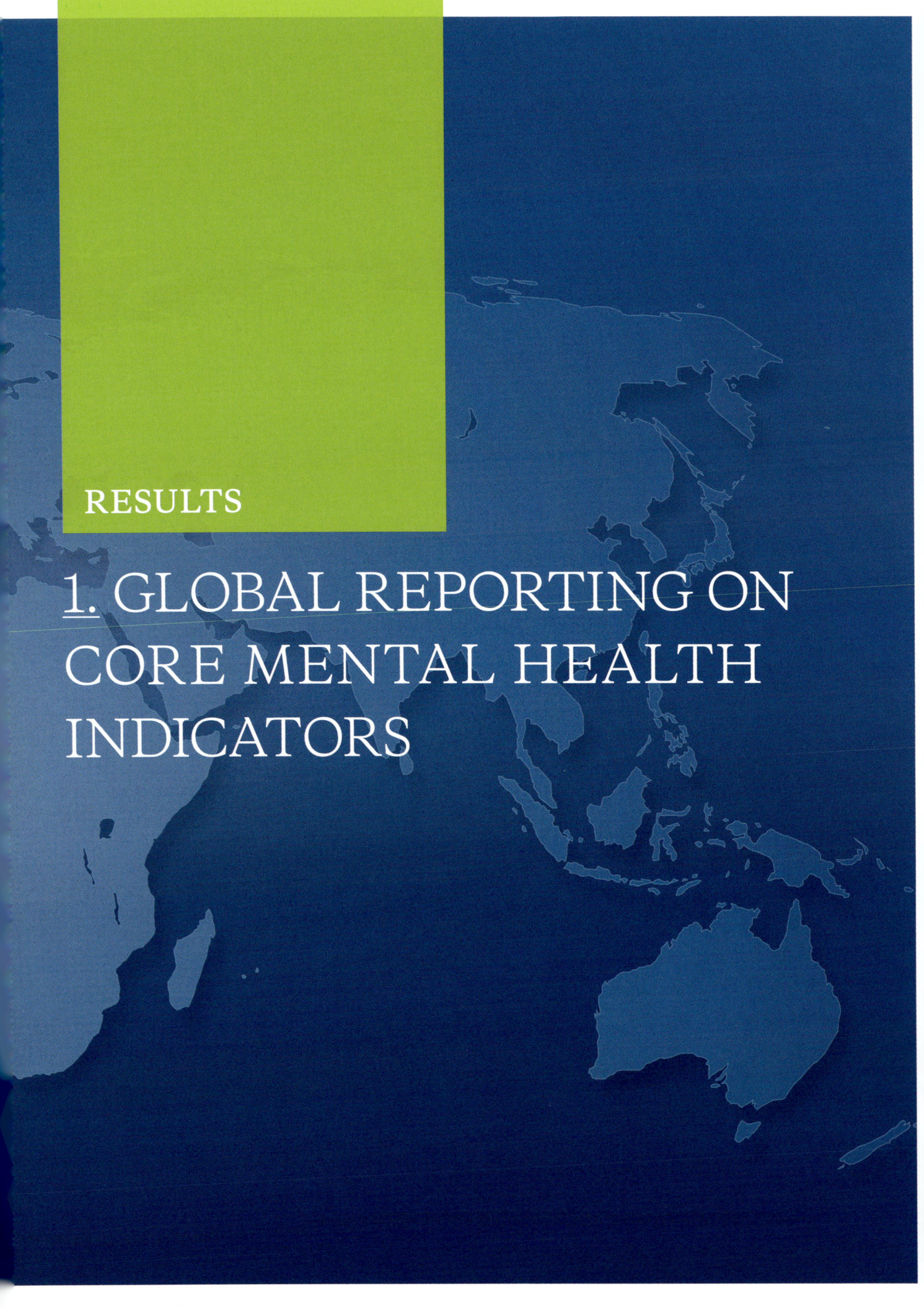

In total, 171 out of WHO's 194 Member States were able to at least partially complete the questionnaire.

As shown in **Figure 1.1**, the global and WHO Regional participation or submission rate for mental health Atlas 2014 exceeded 80% in all WHO Regions and approaches 90% overall. Responding countries account for 97% of the global population (and at least 92% in all WHO Regions). This in itself is an important marker of countries' ability and willingness to collect, share and report their mental health situation.

While reporting levels for many core mental health indicators was high – including those relating to mental health policy and law, workforce and service availability – there was a considerably lower response rate for other indicators, in particular items relating to mental health spending, social support for persons with mental disorders, and service coverage as well as continuity of care for persons with severe mental disorders. The lower response rate for these indicators reflects the difficulty of collecting or obtaining these data, and also the fact that some of these questions were being asked for the first time as part of Atlas.

Accordingly, much effort will be required to reach Target 4 of the Mental Health Action Plan, which states that 80% of countries will be routinely collecting and reporting at least a core set of mental health indicators every two years through their national health and social information systems (by the year 2020). Put another way, the rate of overall completion for successive rounds of Atlas needs to increase considerably over and above what has been achieved in this current round.

Atlas 2014 asked countries to rate the availability or status of mental health reporting; **Figure 1.2** summarises the findings. For those countries responding to this question (155 out of 194, or 80%), 42% are in a position to regularly compile mental health specific data that covers at least the public sector); this is equivalent to 33% of all Member States (42% * 80% response rate). However, nearly 20% of responding countries have not compiled mental health data into any report for policy, planning or management purposes in the last two years. Arranged by World Bank income group, 60% of high-income countries who responded are able to regularly compile mental health specific data that covers at least the public sector, compared to close to 40% of responding countries in other income groups (**Figure 1.3**).

Based on actual data submitted to WHO through Atlas 2014, an assessment of countries' ability to report on a defined set of core mental health indicators was also made. Included indicators were as follows: 1) stand-alone mental health policy or plan (yes or no); 2) stand-alone mental health law (yes or no); 3) mental health workforce (available data for at least some types of worker); 4) service availability (data for at least some care settings); 5) mental health promotion and prevention (completion of inventory, including if no programmes present). 117 countries (60% of all Member States) were able to report on all five of these items. Adding a further key indicator to the defined core set, such as the rate of suicide or service uptake for severe mental disorders, reduces substantially the number of countries able to report, to 91 (47%) and 50 (26%) respectively. This latter, more stringent threshold produces a result quite similar to the one provided above giving the total number of countries who self-reported their ability to regularly compile mental health specific data covering at least the public sector (64 countries, equivalent to 33% of all Member States).

RESULTS
GLOBAL REPORTING ON CORE MENTAL HEALTH INDICATORS

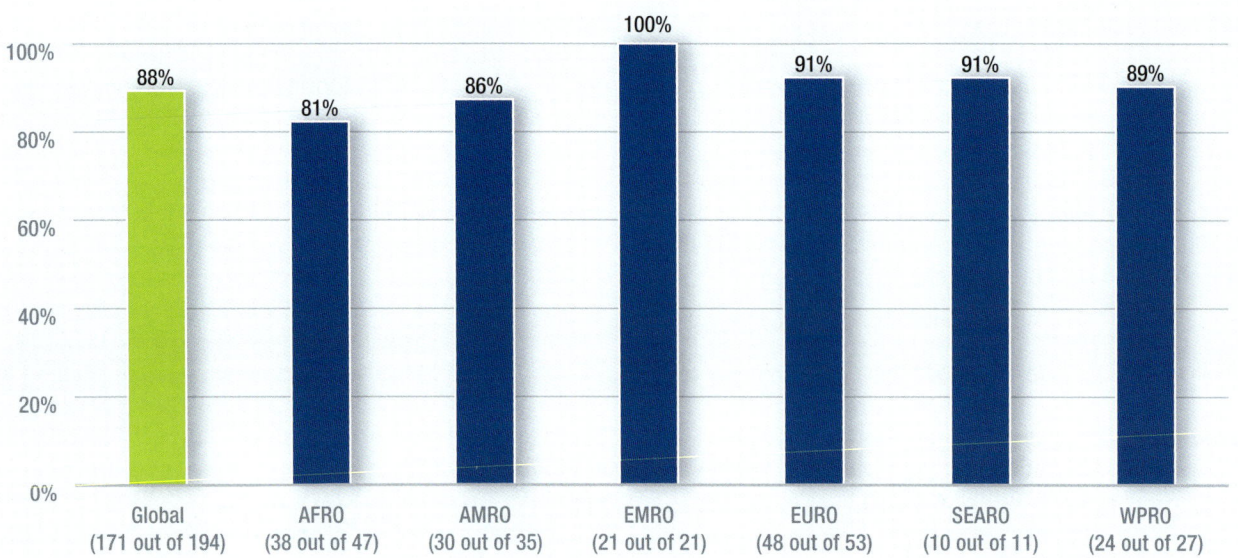

FIG. 1.1 Mental health Atlas 2014: submission rate by Member States

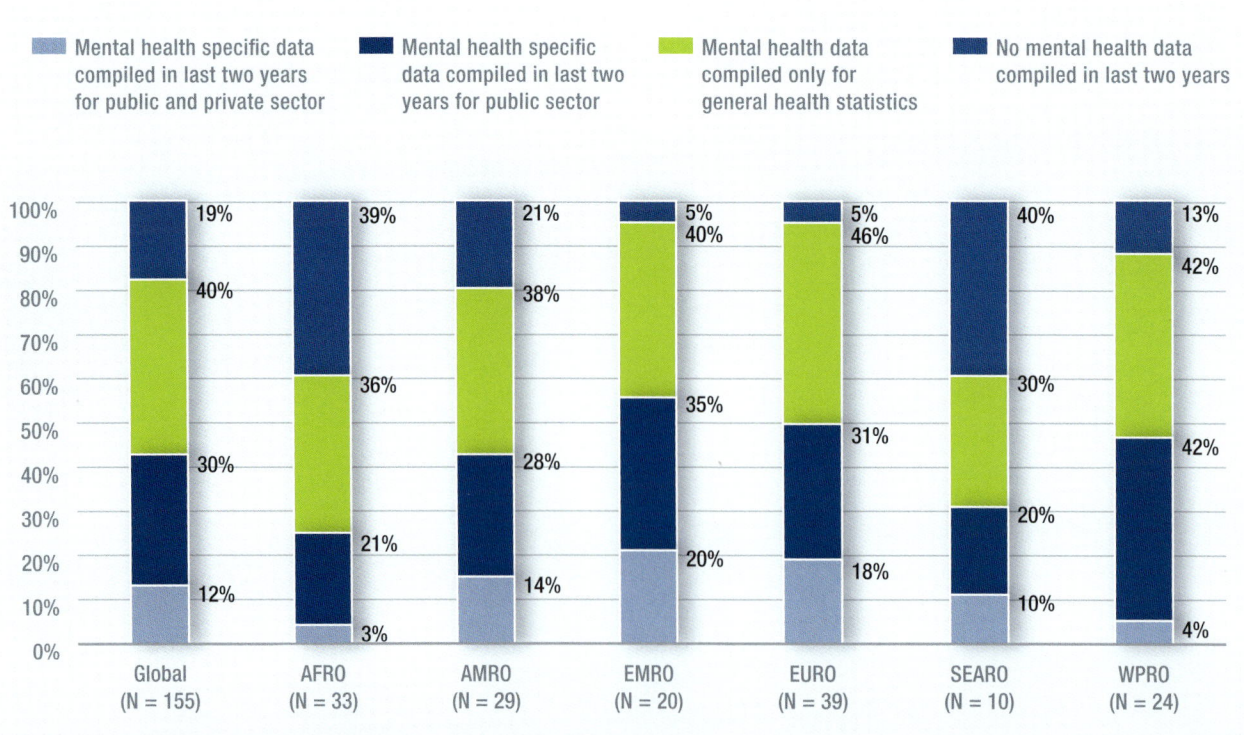

FIG. 1.2 Mental health data availability and reporting, by WHO region

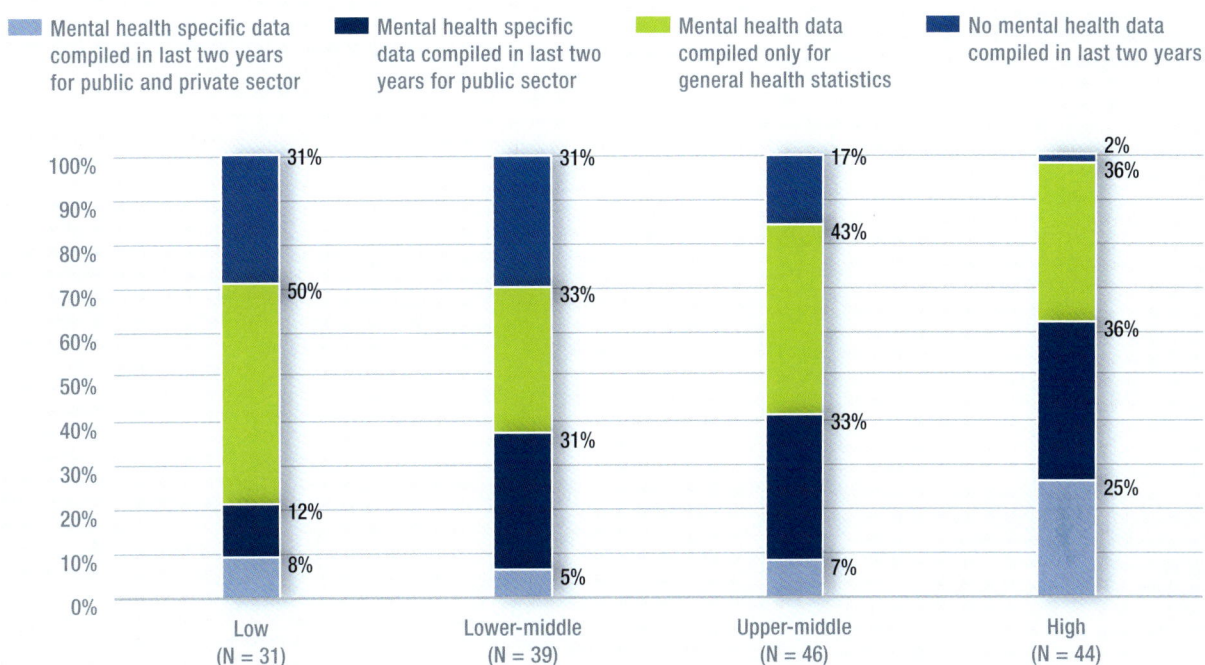

FIG. 1.3 Mental health data availability and reporting, by World Bank income group

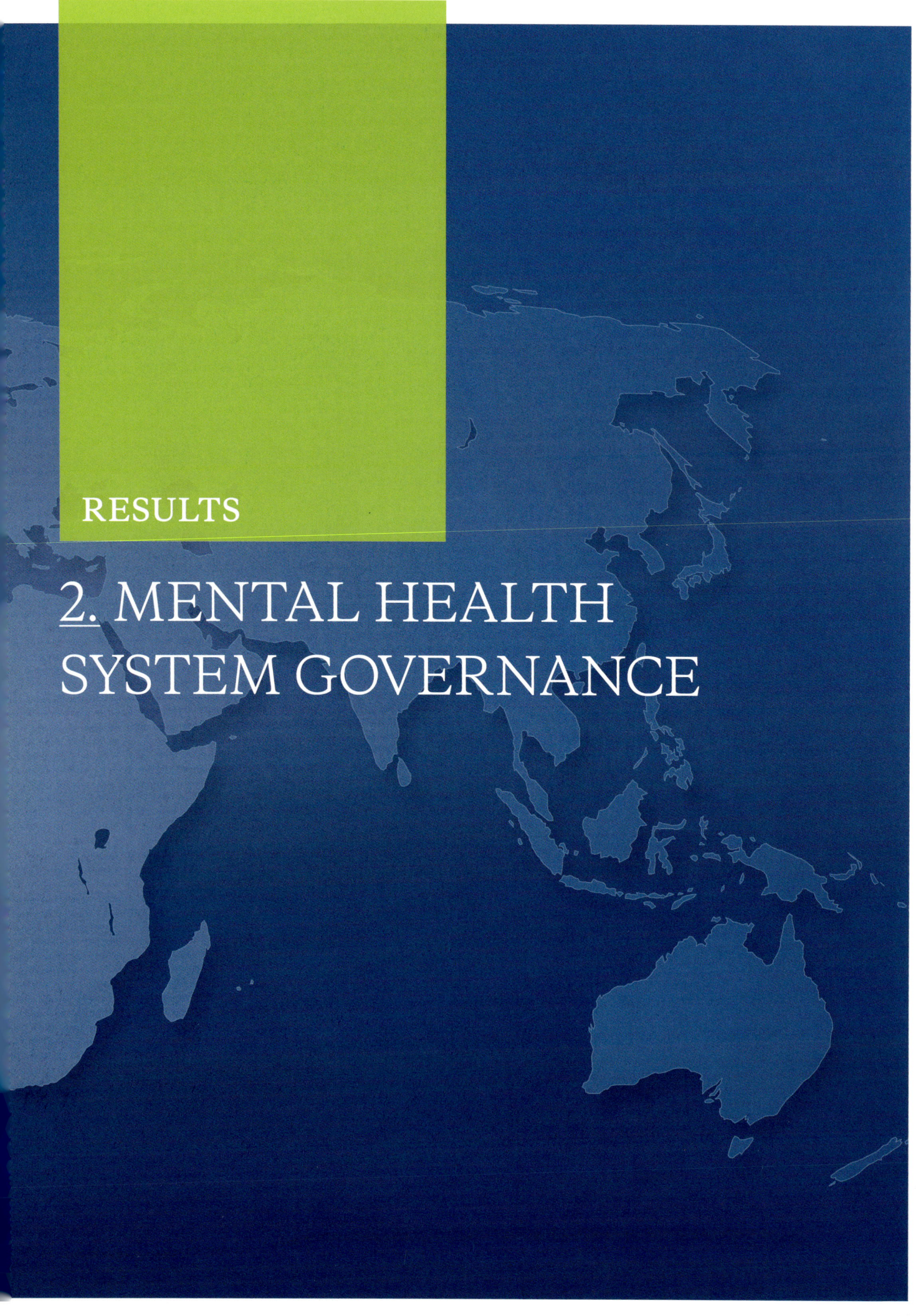

RESULTS

2. MENTAL HEALTH SYSTEM GOVERNANCE

2.1 MENTAL HEALTH POLICIES / PLANS

Objective 1 of the Mental Health Action Plan relates to strengthened leadership and governance for mental health. The articulation and implementation of well-defined mental health policies and plans represent critical ingredients of good governance and leadership. The existence of an explicit mental health policy and plan - whether embedded in other relevant policy/plan documents and/or stand-alone – helps improve the organization and quality of mental health service delivery, accessibility, community care, and the engagement of people with mental disorders as well as their families.

A mental health policy can be broadly defined as an official statement by government or health authority that provides the overall direction for mental health by defining a vision, values, principles and objectives, and by establishing a broad model of action to achieve that vision. A mental health plan details the strategies and activities that will be implemented to realise the vision and achieve the objectives of a mental health policy. It also specifies a budget and timeframe for each strategy and activity, as well as delineating the expected outputs, targets and indicators that can be used to assess whether the implementation of the plan has been successful.

Mental health Atlas 2014 assessed whether countries have an approved mental health policy and/or plan and also the level of its implementation. In addition, and in line with the Mental Health Action Plan, it asked countries to complete a checklist in order to assess the compliance of this mental health policy/plan with international human rights instruments.

In aggregate terms, 131 countries state the existence of a stand-alone policy or plan for mental health, equivalent to 68% of all WHO Member States or 77% of those who submitted a completed Atlas questionnaire and responded to this question (**Table 2.1.1**). The variation between WHO regions is limited, although it can be noted that a rather lower proportion of EMRO countries have policies/plans and a smaller proportion of SEARO countries have updated them. 18 countries have updated their mental health policy / plan in the last year (after 2013), and 81 have done so in the previous five years (since 2010). Out of 37 countries stating that they do not have a stand-alone policy or plan, 21 confirmed that policies and plans for mental health are integrated into those for general health or disability.

The self-rated implementation status of these mental health policies / plans is summarised in **Figure 2.1.1**. A total of 168 Member States responded to this question (higher than for Table 2.1.1 because it includes some countries without a stand-alone policy). It shows that only 15% of responding countries consider themselves to be fully implementing their policy or plan, 14% have a policy / plan but it is not implemented, while a further 10% do not have a policy / plan at all. Most commonly, policies / plans are available but are being partially implemented (61% globally, and between 41% and 77% across the six WHO Regions).

Concerning conformity with international (or regional) human rights instruments, F**igure 2.1.2**. shows the degree of compliance – again, self-rated – across five items of a constructed checklist. More than four out of five countries who responded consider their policy / plan to promote the transition towards mental health services based in the community (including mental health care integrated into general hospitals and primary care), and to pay explicit attention to respect for the human rights of people with mental disorders and psychosocial disabilities. More than two thirds of responding countries consider that their policy / plan fulfils each of three following checklist items: it promotes a full range of services and supports to enable people to live independently and be included in the community; it promotes a recovery approach (including involvement of mental health service users in the development of their treatment and recovery plans); it promotes the participation of persons with mental disorders and psychosocial disabilities in decision making processes on issues affecting them (e.g. policy, law, service reform). Many countries have also made available their policies through online platforms such as WHO's MiNDbank, which enables open assessment of these aspects of national mental health policy.

Using a total score across these five checklist items to evaluate the completeness of the policy in terms of human rights, 80% of responding countries scored at least 3, indicating a partial compliance, while a little over a half endorsed all five items of the checklist, indicating full compliance. The global target to be achieved by 2020 is 80%. **Figure 2.1.3** provides a breakdown by WHO Region; the African and Eastern Mediterranean Regions score lower than other Regions.

RESULTS
MENTAL HEALTH SYSTEM GOVERNANCE

WHO regions	Countries stating they have a stand-alone mental health policy / plan		Countries stating they have updated their policy / plan in last 5 years (since 2010)	
	Number	% of responders	Number	% of responders
Global	**131**	**77%**	**81**	**47%**
AFRO	27	71%	16	42%
AMRO	24	80%	13	43%
EMRO	14	67%	11	52%
EURO	38	79%	27	56%
SEARO	8	80%	3	30%
WPRO	20	83%	11	46%

TABLE 2.1.1 Existence and revision status of stand-alone mental health policies / plans

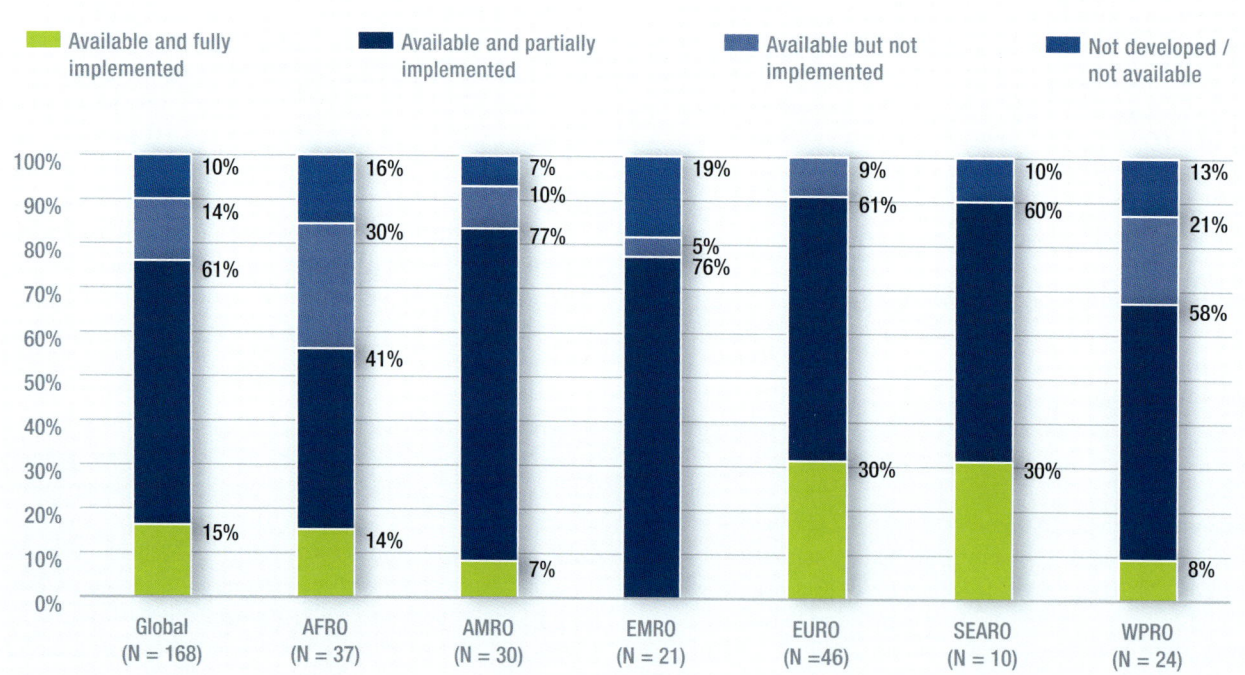

FIG. 2.1.1 Implementation status of mental health policies / plans

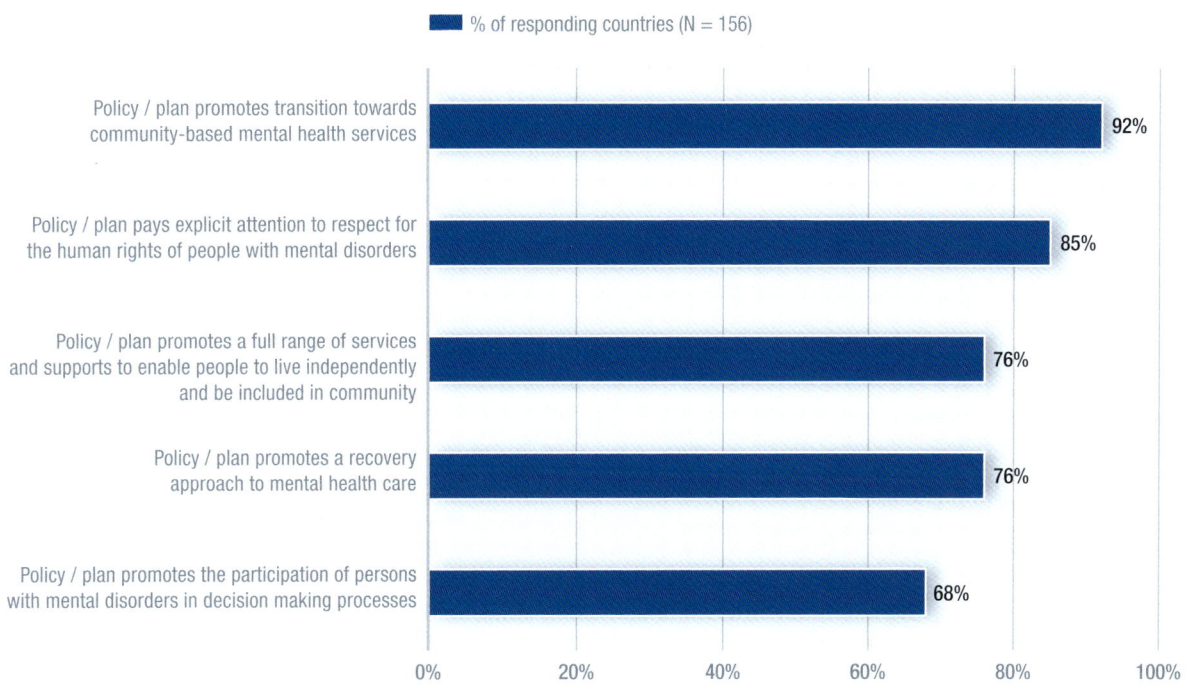

FIG. 2.1.2 Compliance of mental health policies / plans with human rights instruments

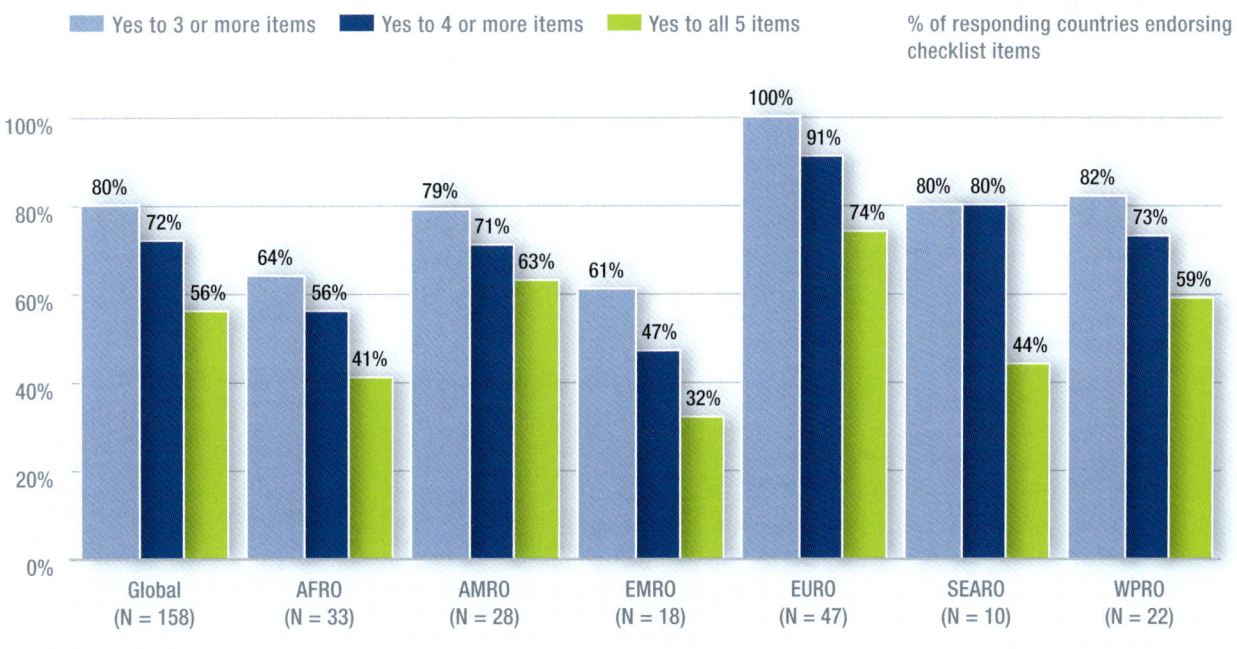

FIG. 2.1.3 Mental health policies / plans and human rights: checklist score

RESULTS
MENTAL HEALTH SYSTEM GOVERNANCE

2.2 MENTAL HEALTH LEGISLATION

Mental health legislation is a further key component of good governance, and concerns the specific legal provisions that are primarily related to mental health. Such legislation typically focuses on issues such as human rights protections for people with mental disorders, involuntary admission and treatment, guardianship, professional training and service structure.

Mental health Atlas 2014 assessed whether countries have a stand-alone mental health law, and the extent to which legislation is currently being used or implemented. As with mental health policy / plans, a checklist was developed and used to assess the degree to which laws fall in line with international human rights instruments.

A total of 99 countries report having a stand-alone law for mental health, which represents 51% of WHO Member States and 63% of those who submitted a response (**Table 2.2.1**). The European and Western Pacific Regions have the highest percentage (over 70%), while the African and American Regions have the lowest (50-55%). 31 countries have updated their mental health legislation in the previous five years (since 2010), again most commonly in the European and Western Pacific Regions; in the African and American Regions, less than 10% of responding countries have updated their laws. Out of the 68 countries stating that they do not have a stand-alone law for mental health, 47 have mental health legislation that is integrated into general health or disability law (while 21 do not).

The self-rated implementation status of mental health legislation across WHO regions – whether or not stand-alone laws for mental health are in place – is shown in **Figure 2.2.1**. A higher total of 165 Member States responded to this question. 16% of responding countries state that mental health legislation is not yet developed or available (inter-regional range: 0-35%), and a further 10% state that legislation is available but not acted upon. However, 31% of countries judge themselves to be fully implementing their mental health laws, which is a higher rate of full implementation than seen for mental health policies / plans. In the European Region the rate exceeds 60%; by contrast, none of the countries in the South East Asian Region score themselves as fully implementing their laws. Again, the most commonly stated response is a partial implementation of existing laws (inter-regional range: 36-57%).

Regarding conformity with international (or regional) human rights instruments, **Figure 2.2.2** shows positive responses to five items of a checklist constructed for this purpose. Between 60-75% of countries who responded consider their laws to: a) promote the transition towards mental health services based in the community (including mental health care integrated into general hospitals and primary care); b) promote the rights of persons with mental disorders and psychosocial disabilities to exercise their legal capacity; c) promote alternatives to coercive practice; d) provide for procedures to enable people with mental disorders and psychosocial disabilities to protect their rights and file appeals and complaints to an independent legal body; and e) provide for regular inspections of human rights conditions in mental health facilities by an independent body.

Adding up these endorsed checklist items provides a measure of the extent to which countries consider their mental health laws to be partially or fully in line with international human rights instruments (**Figure 2.2.3**). 68% of responding countries endorsed at least 3 checklist items, and 42% endorsed all five items. The lower expected rate of conformity of mental health laws with international human rights instruments (compared to mental health policies and plans) is reflected in Global Target 1.2 of the Mental Health Action Plan, which states that 50% of countries will have developed or updated their law for mental health in line with international and regional human rights instruments by the year 2020.

WHO regions	Countries stating they have a stand-alone mental health law		Countries stating they have updated their legislation in last 5 years	
	Number	% of responders	Number	% of responders
Global	**99**	**63%**	**31**	**18%**
AFRO	18	55%	1	3%
AMRO	14	50%	2	7%
EMRO	12	67%	5	24%
EURO	33	70%	12	25%
SEARO	6	60%	2	20%
WPRO	16	73%	9	38%

TABLE 2.2.1   Existence and revision status of mental health legislation

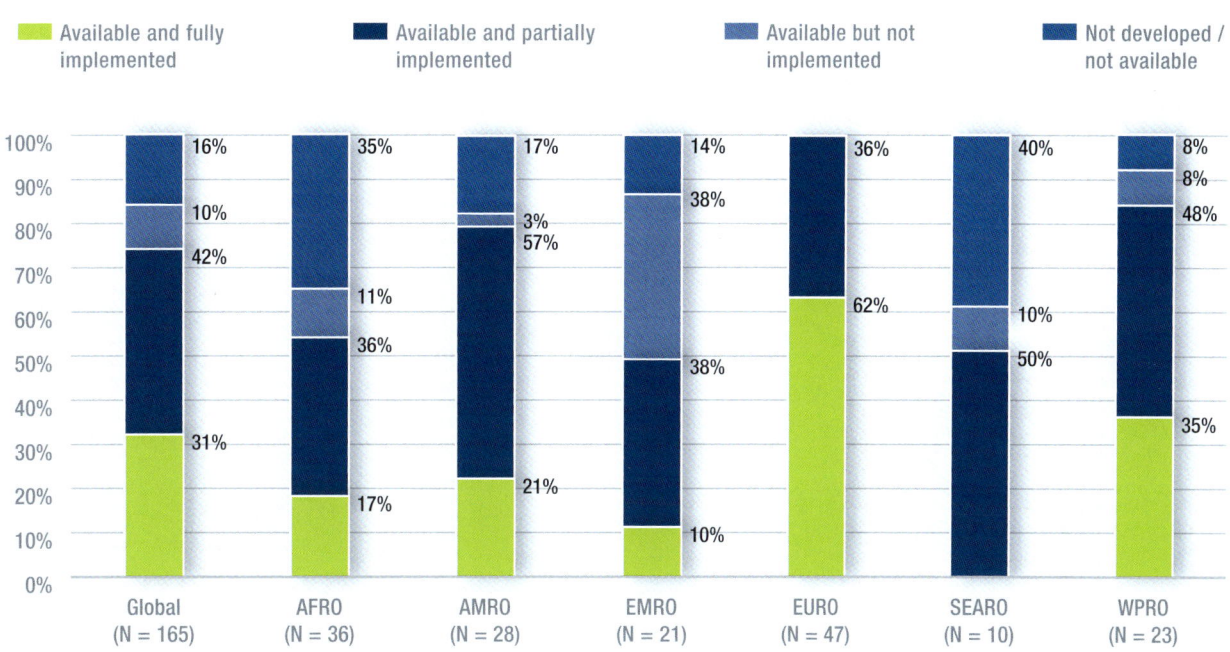

FIG. 2.2.1 Implementation status of mental health legislation

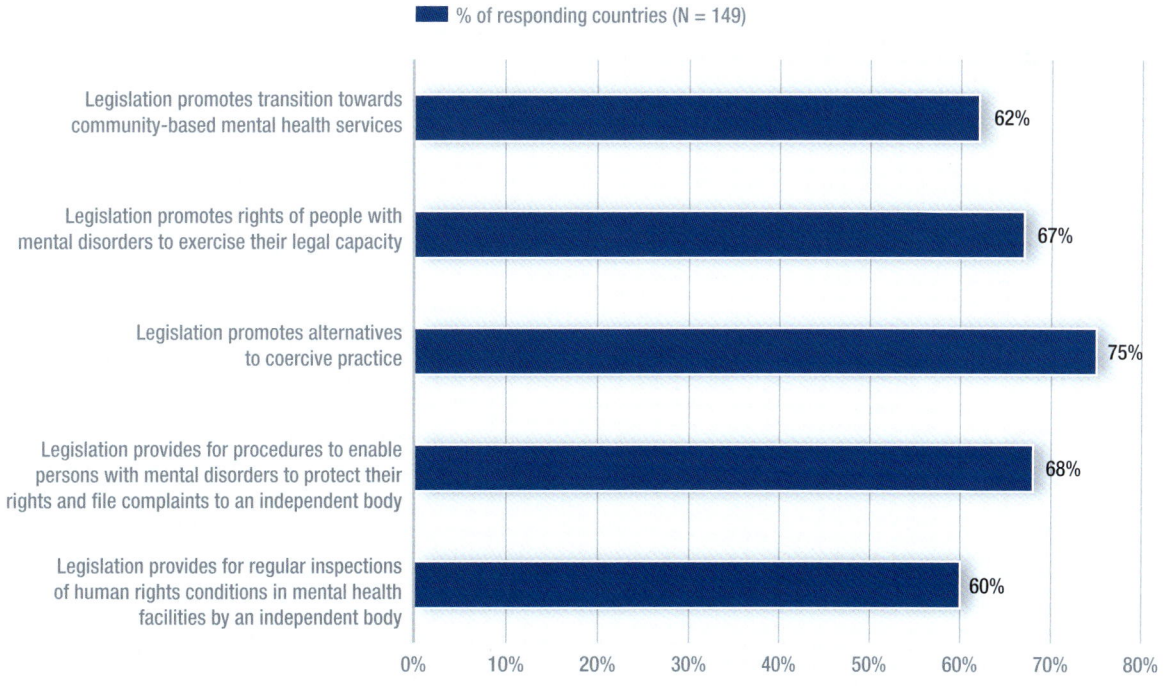

FIG. 2.2.2 Compliance of mental health legislation with human rights instruments

RESULTS
MENTAL HEALTH SYSTEM GOVERNANCE

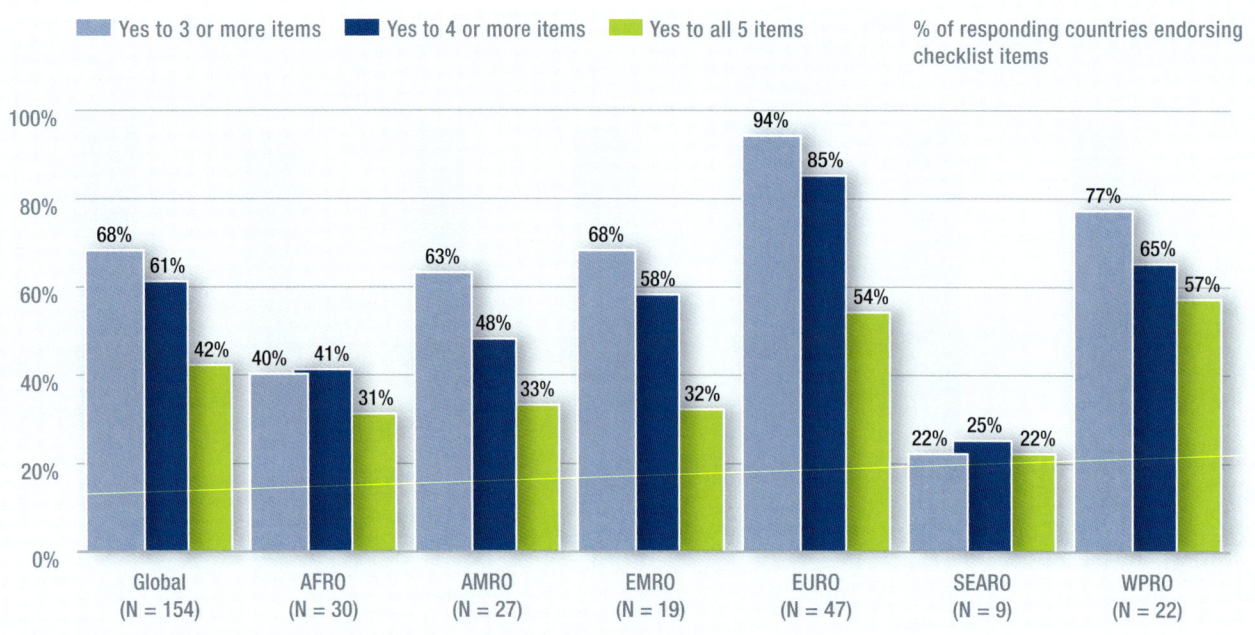

FIG. 2.2.3 Mental health legislation and human rights: checklist score

2.3 STAKEHOLDER INVOLVEMENT

In addition to the participation item in the mental health policy checklist, a separate checklist was constructed in order to assess the level of involvement of associations of persons with mental disorders and family members in the formulation and implementation of mental health policies, laws and services at national level (in the previous two years).

The checklist included measures relating to: the availability of information about organizations of persons with mental disorders and psychosocial disabilities, and of families and carers; a Ministry of Health policy on participation; early involvement of persons with mental disorders and psychosocial disabilities, as well as families and carers, in mental health policy and legislation development; participation in government committees concerned with mental health policy and service development; and availability of resources for participation and reimbursement of associated costs.

Global findings relating to a number of domains of involvement are provided in **Figure 2.3.1**. Out of 149 countries who responded, no more than 20% consider themselves to be fully implementing the specified measures, and for each domain there is no implementation in at least one third of countries.

As shown in **Figure 2.3.2**, there is appreciable variation in the extent of involvement across WHO regions, with the American, European and South East Asian Regions exhibiting higher levels of participation, while the African and Eastern Mediterranean Regions have lower levels.

MENTAL HEALTH ATLAS 2014

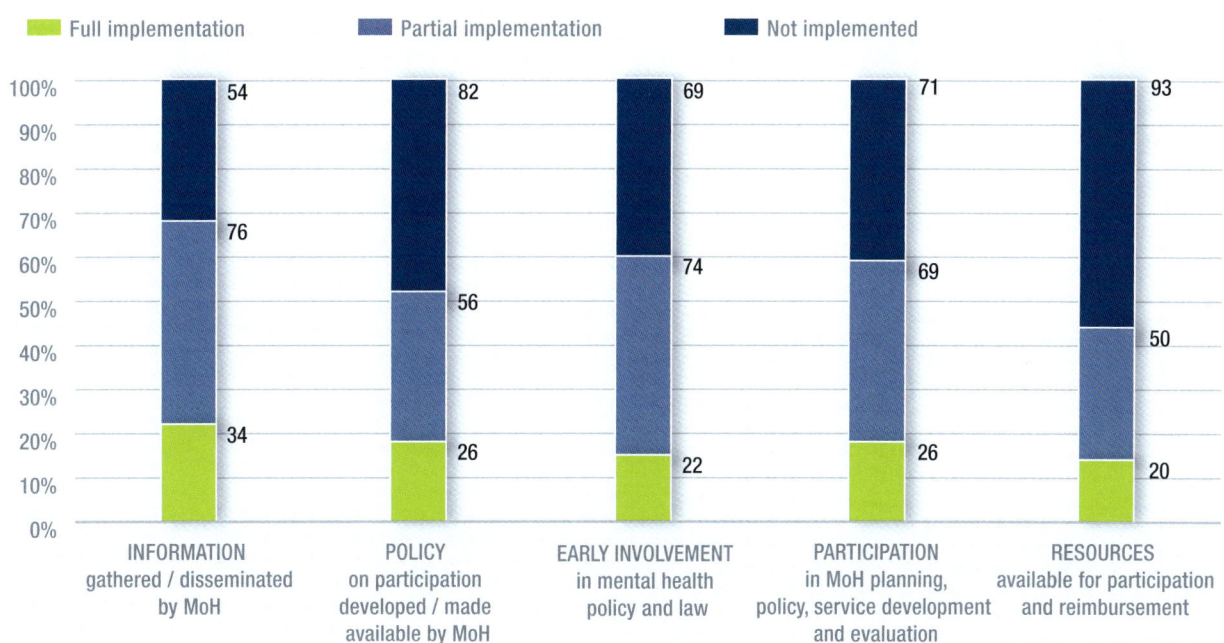

FIG. 2.3.1 Involvement of persons with mental disorders and family members in the formulation and implementation of mental health policies, laws and services (numeric values alongside the bars are number of countries)

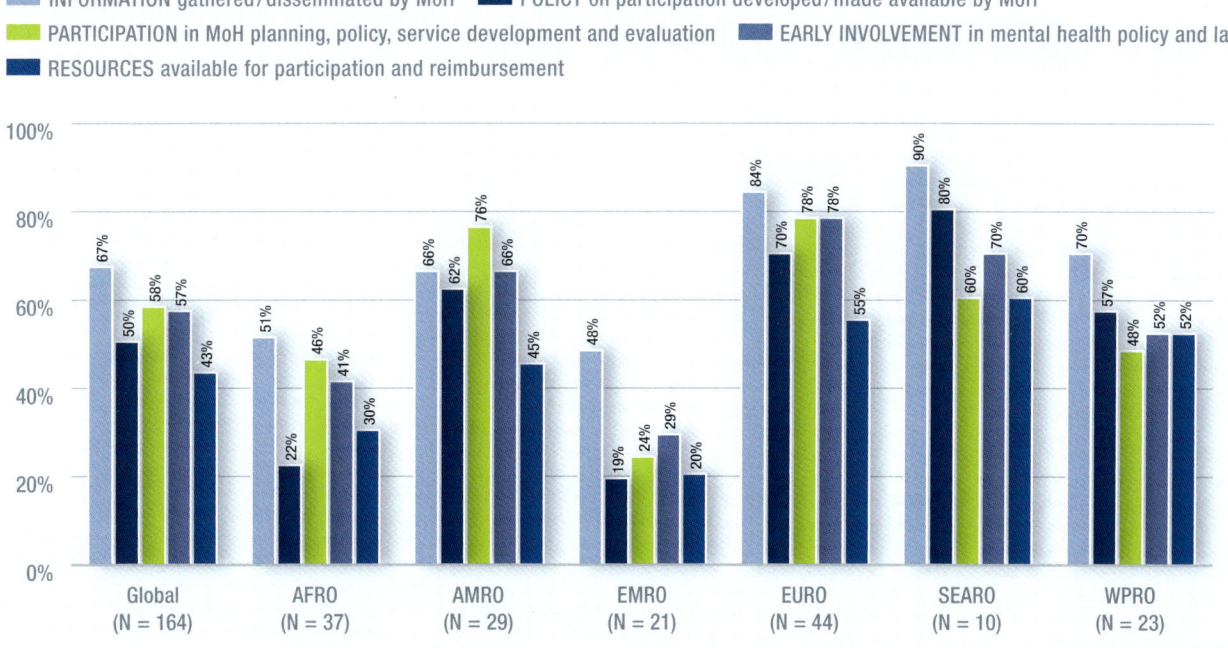

FIG. 2.3.2 Partial or full involvement of persons with mental disorders and family members in mental health policies, laws and service development, by WHO region
(% of responding countries that are partially or fully implementing stakeholder involvement)

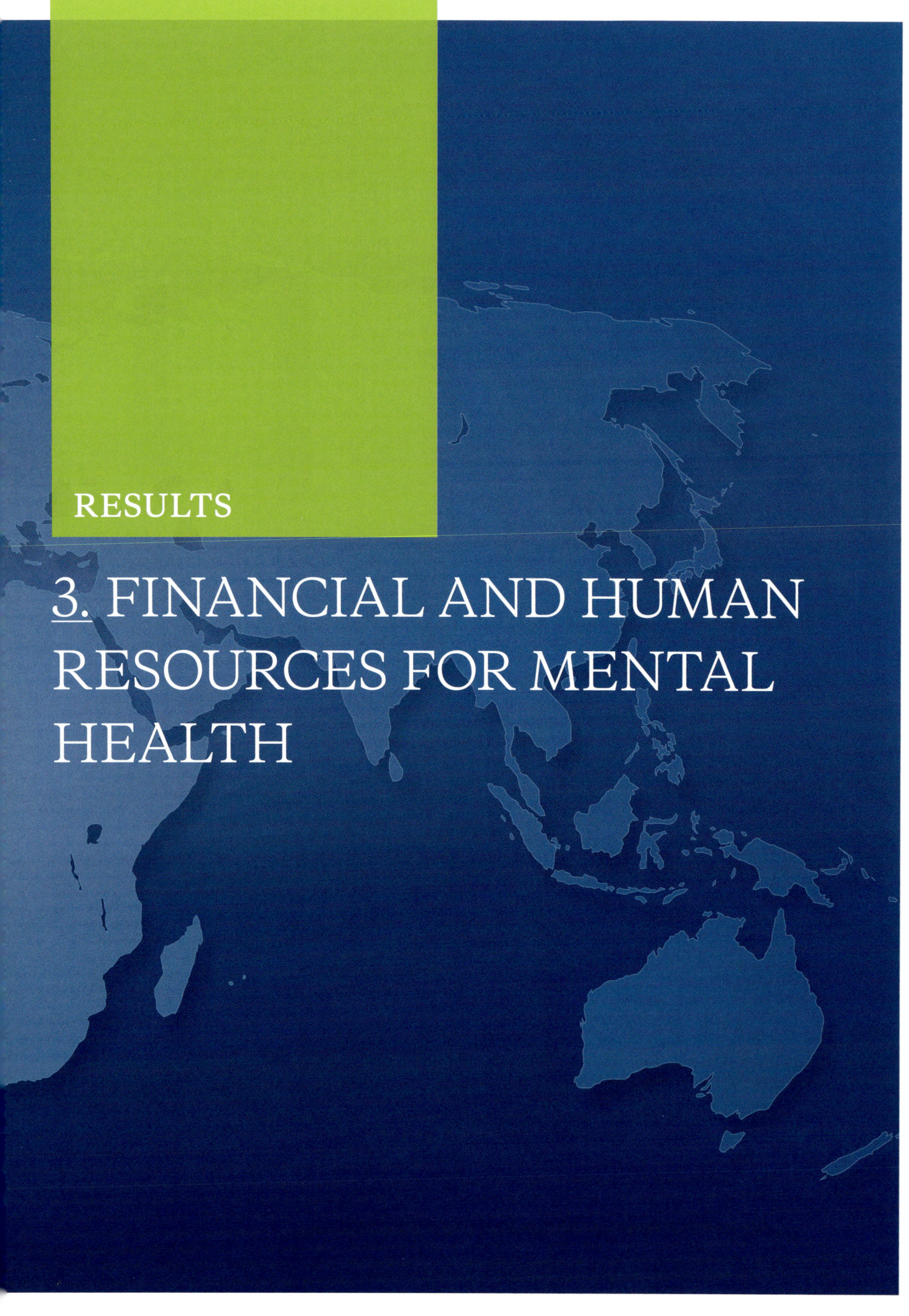

RESULTS

3. FINANCIAL AND HUMAN RESOURCES FOR MENTAL HEALTH

3.1 GOVERNMENT MENTAL HEALTH SPENDING

Financial resources are an evident requirement for developing and maintaining mental health services and moving towards programme goals (including increased service coverage for identified populations in need). Estimation of mental health expenditure in a country, however, is complex, due to the range of funding sources (employers and households as well as governmental or non-governmental agencies) and also the diverse set of service providers (specialist mental health services, general health services and social care services).

In Atlas 2014, countries were asked to first rank the most important sources of funding, with particular focus on care and treatment of severe mental disorders. **Table 3.1.1** shows the first and second most highly ranked funding source, both for each WHO Region and also by World Bank income status.

The results demonstrate that Government is by far the most commonly cited main source of funds (first ranked in 79% of the 120 countries responding to this item; inter-regional range: 67-100%). In 18% of countries, however, households are ranked as the main source of funds (mainly through direct out-of-pocket payments, but could also be via private health insurance cover). Non-governmental organizations and employers were barely ever ranked first, but both were frequently ranked as the second most important source of funds (22% and 31% of responding countries, respectively). Since households were also commonly ranked second (31% of responding countries), this indicates a very mixed picture in terms of non-governmental contributions to the financing of mental health services. The finding that households are ranked as first in 18% of countries and first or second in half the countries raises particular concerns regarding the fairness of financial contributions and equitable access to services, especially for lower-income households.

Countries were also requested to estimate total government spending in the last year, broken down by care setting (inpatient and day care services; outpatient and primary health care services; social care services; and other programmatic expenditures). Over 60 countries were able to provide at least some expenditure information – most commonly in relation to mental hospitals – but only 41 countries were able to report both inpatient and outpatient expenditures. Even less countries were able to report on spending incurred at the level of primary care facilities and clinics, even though this represents a crucial aspect of mental health service provision in the community.

Based on this reduced sample and the incomplete data that countries were able to provide (e.g. on primary health care or social care services), **Figure 3.1.1** depicts median government mental health spending per capita for countries at different levels of income. Expenditure levels in low, lower-middle and upper-middle income country groups is very low (less than US$ 2), and falls far below levels estimated for high-income countries (over US$ 50 per head of population). As shown in **Figure 3.1.2**, much of the reported expenditure is allocated to inpatient care, and to mental hospitals in particular.

The strong association between income level and public mental health spending is shown in **Figure 3.1.3**, which plots total government mental health spending per capita against gross national income (GNI) per capita. Just over 50% of the observed variance is explained by this association (which increases to 65% when three low-population but very high-income countries are excluded). Across all country income groups, reported mental health spending represents less than 5% of general government health expenditures. Out of the sample of 41 countries, only seven allocated more than 5%. **Figure 3.1.4** shows the relationship between total government spending as a proportion of total health spending and GNI per capita; the explained level or variance is less strong than that shown in Figure 3.1.3.

WHO regions	N	Government (national insurance)		NGOs (for profit or not for profit)		Employers (social health insurance)		Households (private insurance, out-of pocket)	
		First ranked	Second ranked	First ranked	Second ranked	First ranked	Second ranked	First ranked	Second ranked
Global	122	79%	14%	2%	22%	2%	33%	18%	31%
AFRO	28	67%	19%	4%	30%	7%	30%	22%	22%
AMRO	25	78%	13%	0%	26%	0%	48%	22%	13%
EMRO	14	77%	15%	8%	23%	0%	23%	15%	38%
EURO	32	86%	14%	0%	14%	0%	26%	14%	46%
SEARO	10	100%	0%	0%	22%	0%	44%	0%	33%
WPRO	13	77%	15%	0%	15%	0%	38%	23%	31%

TABLE 3.1.1 Main source of funds for care and treatment of severe mental disorders

RESULTS
FINANCIAL AND HUMAN RESOURCES FOR MENTAL HEALTH

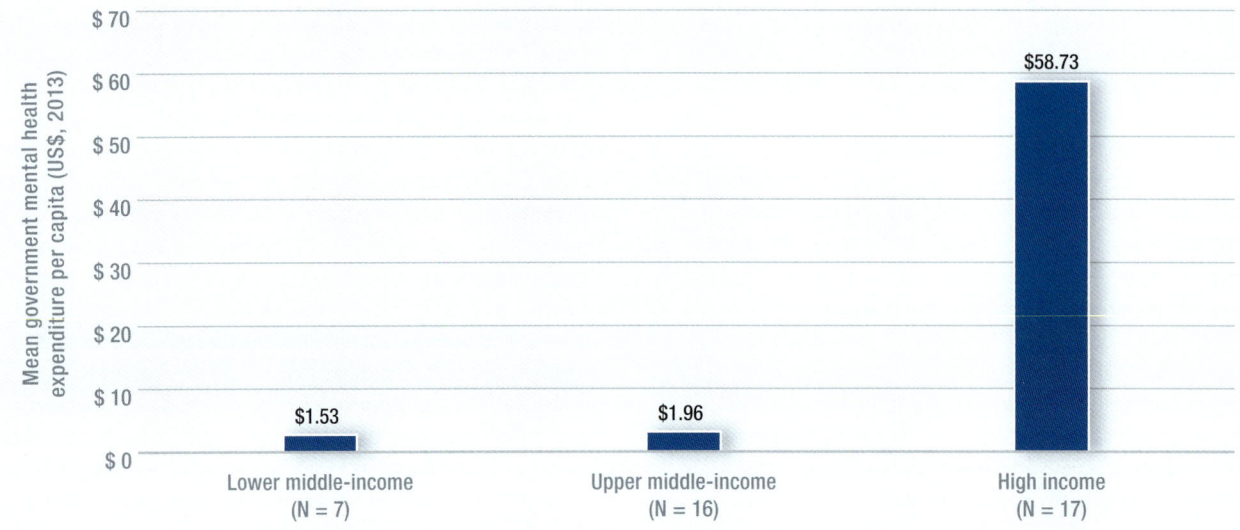

FIG. 3.1.1   Median mental health expenditure per capita, by World Bank income group

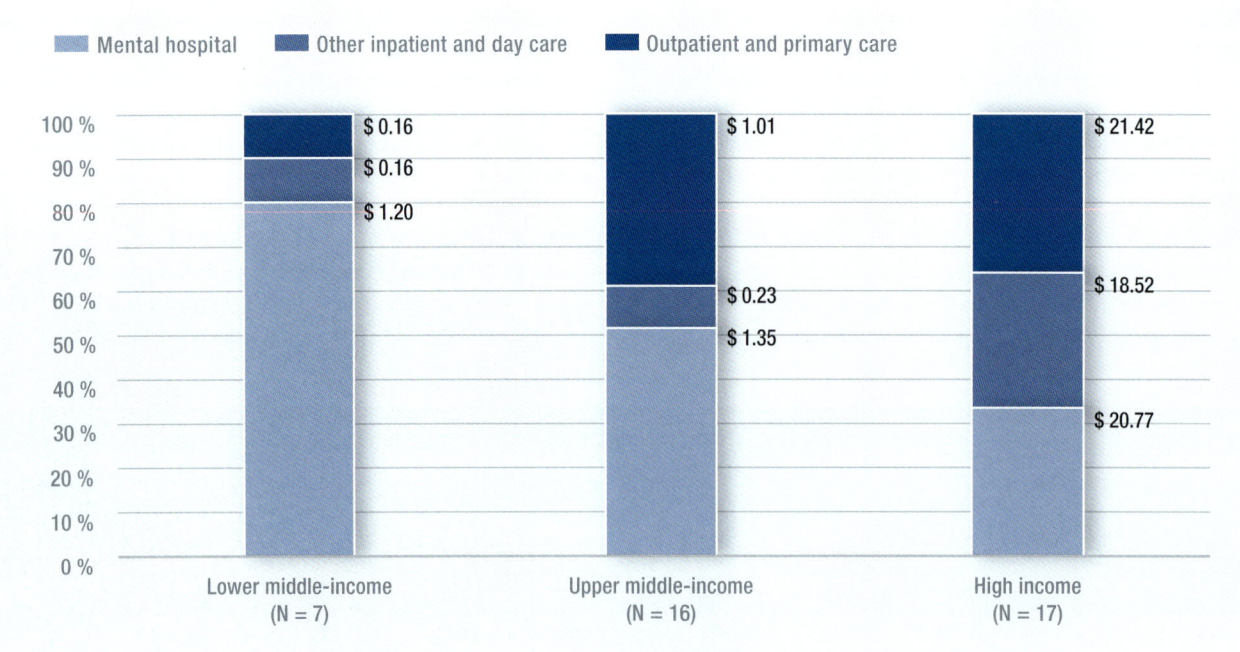

FIG. 3.1.2   Distribution of mental health expenditure per capita, by care setting

Note: Low-income countries not represented due to low sample size (N=1).

MENTAL HEALTH ATLAS 2014

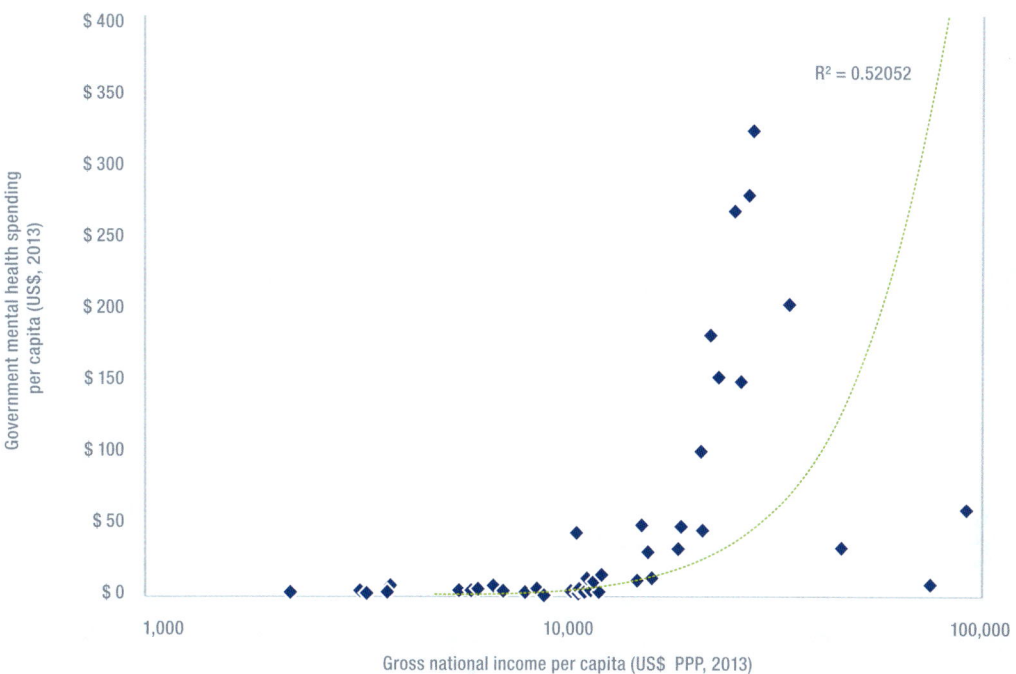

FIG. 3.1.3 Association between mental health expenditure per capita and gross national income (N = 41)

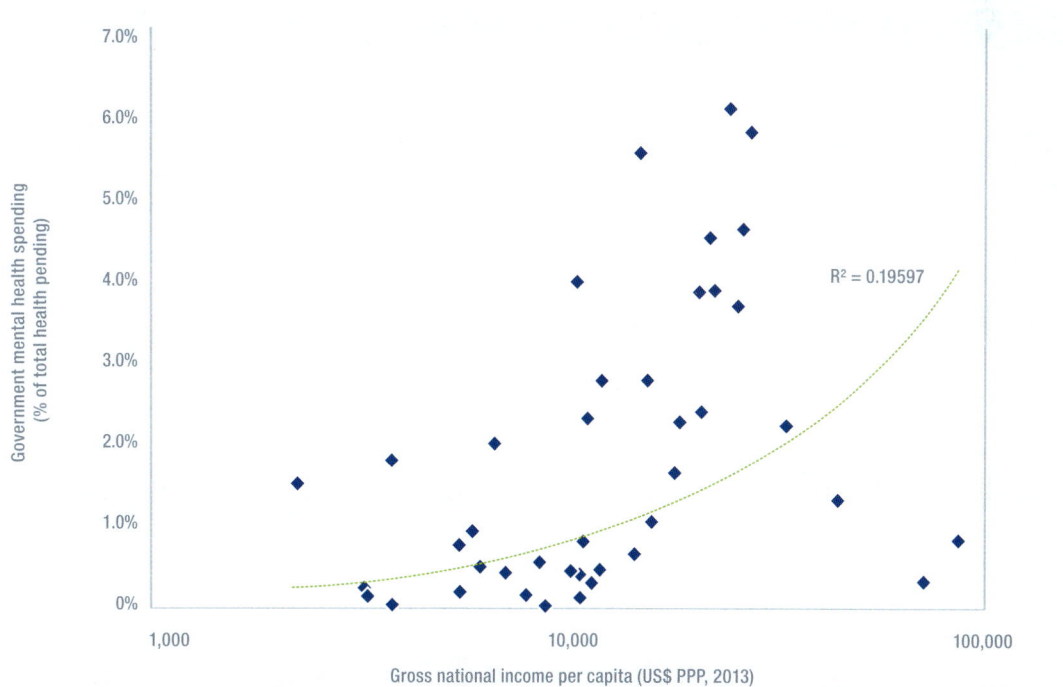

FIG. 3.1.4 Association between mental health expenditure (as a percentage of total health expenditure) and gross national income (N = 41)

RESULTS
FINANCIAL AND HUMAN RESOURCES FOR MENTAL HEALTH

3.2 MENTAL HEALTH TRAINING IN PRIMARY HEALTH CARE

The training of primary care staff in mental health is a critical issue for the capacity of this sector to recognize and to treat persons with severe and common mental disorders. Countries were requested to report the *total* number of primary care staff – broken down by profession – who were trained in mental health for at least two days in the last two years. These reported numbers were then divided by WHO estimates of the total workforce of doctors, nurses and community health workers in each country (that is, not just those working in primary care).

Based on a sample of 67 countries able to provide figures, it is estimated globally that a median of just over 2% of physicians and 1.8% of nurses and midwives received at least two days training in mental health in the previous two years (**Table 3.2.1**). A noteworthy finding is that a higher proportion of nurses and midwives have received this level of training in low-income countries than in other income groups.

3.3 MENTAL HEALTH WORKFORCE

As with earlier Atlas surveys, countries were requested to provide estimates of the total number of mental health professionals working in the country, broken down by specific occupation (including psychiatrists, other medical doctors, nurses, psychologists, social workers, occupational therapists and other paid workers working in mental health). A total of 130 countries, representing two-thirds of all WHO Member States, were able to provide at least partial estimates of known mental health workers in their country, in many cases also broken down by care setting (which here excluded non-specialised health professionals working in general health facilities or services). The median number of mental health workers per 100,000 population are shown for different WHO regions and for countries at different income levels in **Figure 3.3.1** and **Figure 3.3.2**, respectively. Based on these reported data, rates are estimated to vary from below 1 per 100,000 population in low-income countries to over 50 in high-income countries. The global median is 9 per 100,000 population, or less than one mental health worker for every 10,000 people.

	Physicians		Nurses and midwives	
	N	%	N	%
Global	67	2.1%	65	1.8%
WHO region				
AFRO	13	0.6%	19	4.0%
AMRO	17	2.4%	17	2.4%
EMRO	12	2.7%	7	1.6%
EURO	9	2.0%	5	0.8%
SEARO	6	1.4%	6	2.5%
WPRO	10	3.4%	11	0.9%
Income group				
High	11	3.1%	6	1.2%
Upper-middle	24	1.9%	22	1.9%
Lower-middle	25	2.4%	26	1.7%
Low	7	2.8%	11	6.7%

TABLE 3.2.1 Mental health training of physician and nurses, by WHO Region and World Bank income group

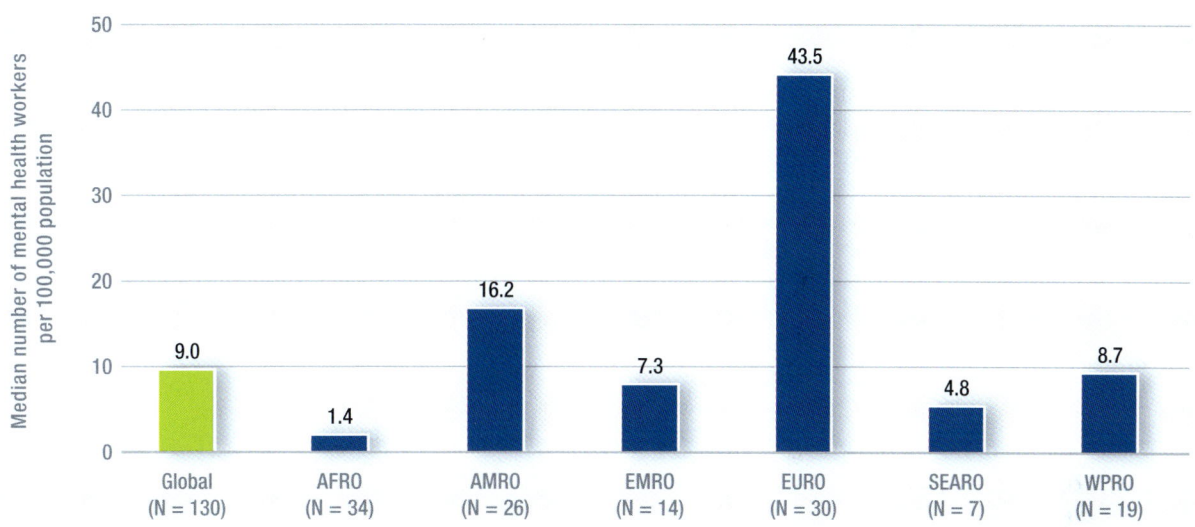

FIG. 3.3.1 Mental health workforce per 100,000 population, by WHO region

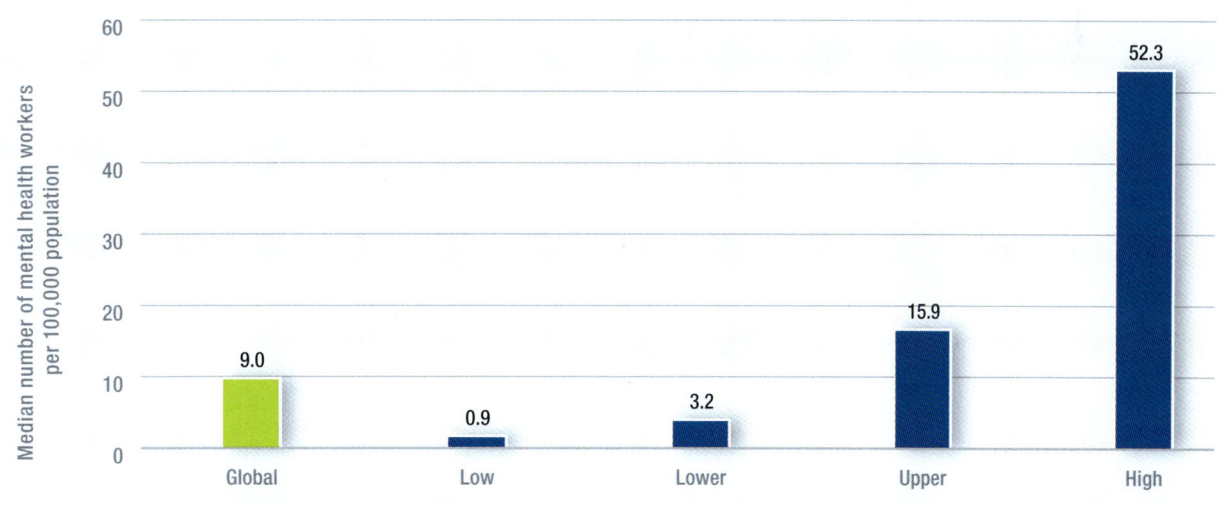

FIG. 3.3.2 Mental health workforce per 100,000 population, by World Bank income group

RESULTS
FINANCIAL AND HUMAN RESOURCES FOR MENTAL HEALTH

Figures 3.3.3-3.3.4 provide a breakdown of the composition of this workforce, again by WHO region and income group (exact values are only shown for the largest categories of worker). Results indicate that the proportion of different staff categories is quite stable across countries at different income levels, with nurses comprising the single largest group of workers (40-60%). However, the absolute number of workers per 100,000 population varies enormously; for example, there are 6.6 psychiatrists per 100,000 population in the sampled high-income countries, compared to less than 0.5 per 100,000 population in low- and lower-middle income countries. Similarly, there are over 30 nurses working in mental health per 100,000 population in high-income country settings compared to 0.4 in low-income countries, 2.5 in lower-middle-income countries and 7.1 in upper-middle income countries.

A breakdown by care setting was also derived. Figure 3.3.5 shows the proportion of the total mental health workforce allocated to inpatient and day care services on the one hand, and outpatient care services on the other hand. Across all WHO regions, the large majority of mental health workers counted in the Atlas 2014 survey are working in inpatient and day care services (82% globally).

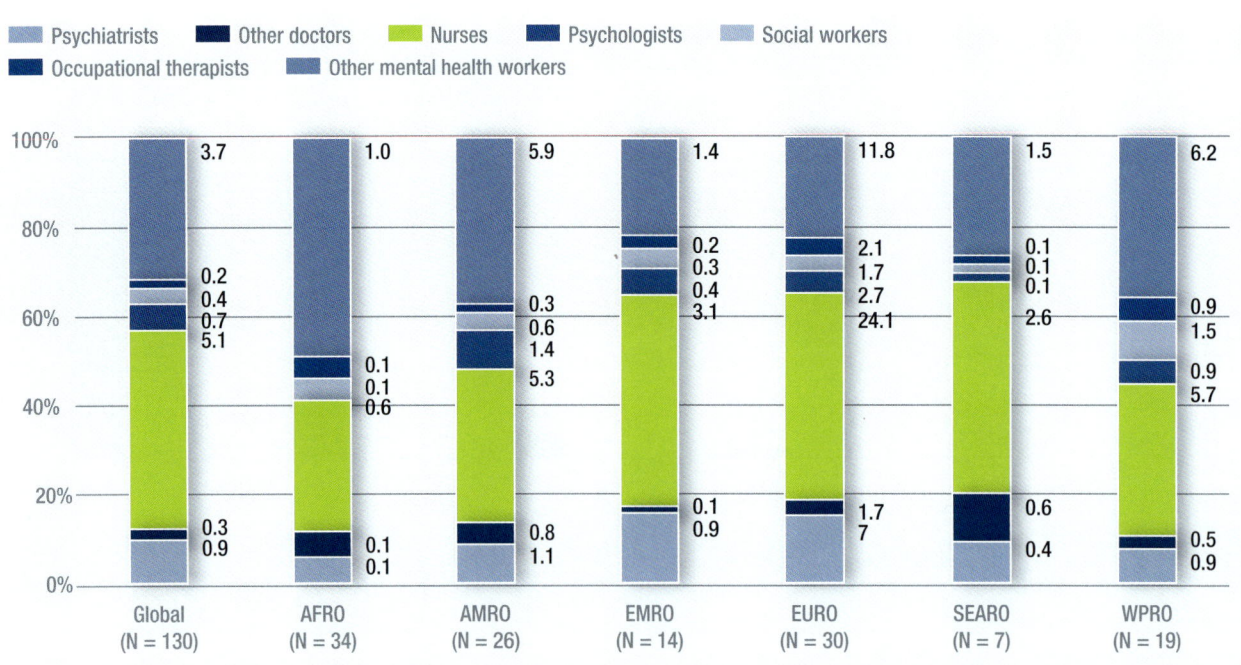

FIG. 3.3.3 Mental health workforce breakdown, by WHO region
(numeric values alongside the bars are health worker rates per 100,000 population)

MENTAL HEALTH ATLAS 2014

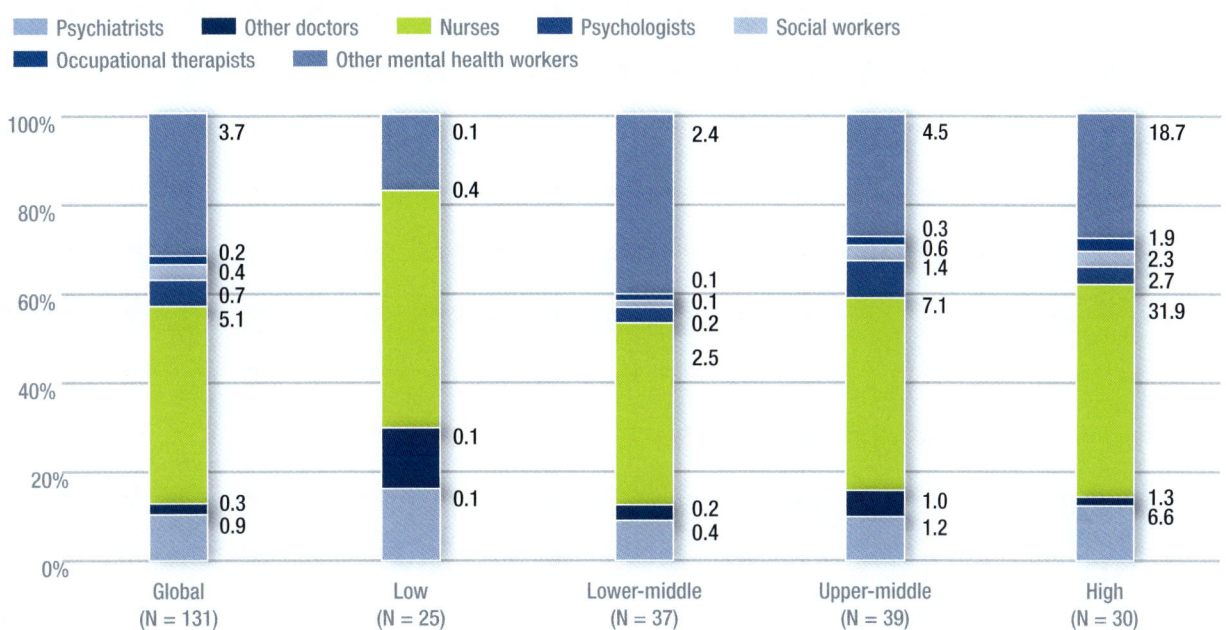

FIG. 3.3.4 Mental health workforce breakdown, by World Bank income group
(values alongside the bars are health worker rates per 100,000 population)

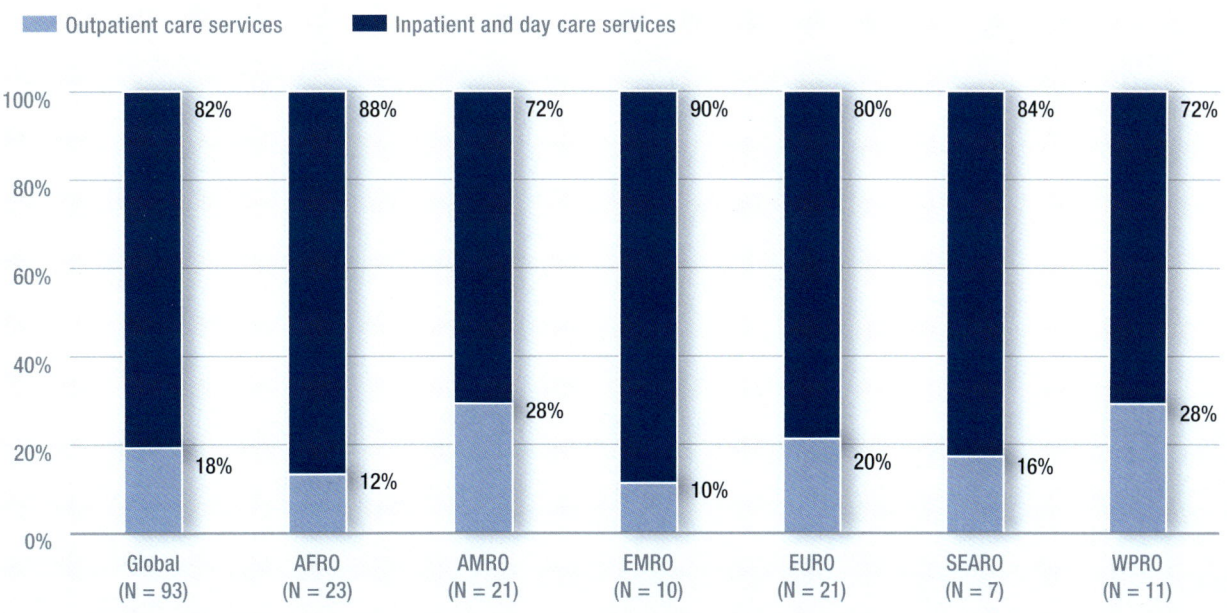

FIG. 3.3.5 Proportion of mental health workforce providing inpatient and outpatient services, by WHO Region

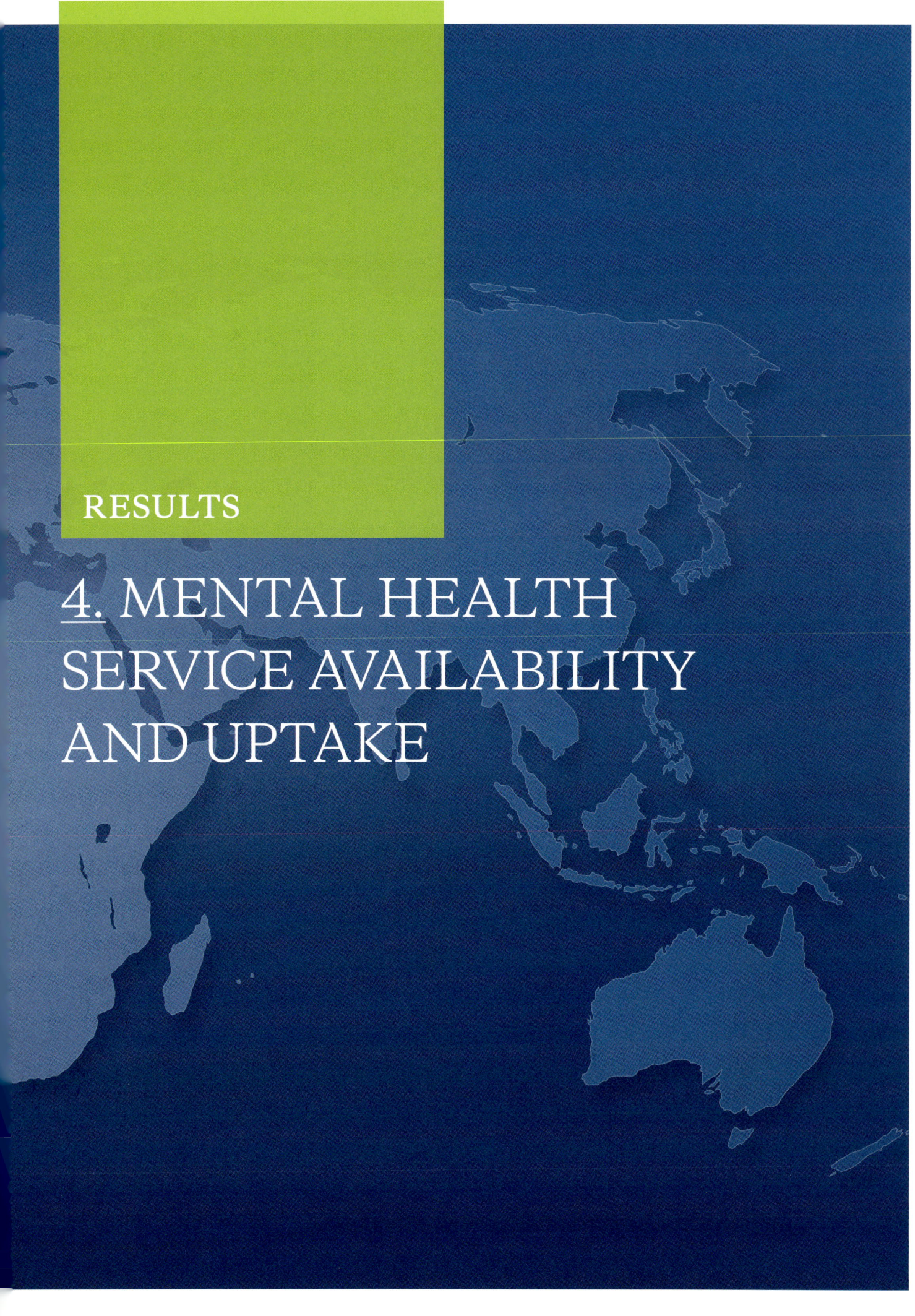

RESULTS

4. MENTAL HEALTH SERVICE AVAILABILITY AND UPTAKE

4.1 INPATIENT AND RESIDENTIAL CARE

Inpatient and residential care is composed of mental hospitals, psychiatric wards in general hospitals, community residential facilities and other residential facilities. Definitions of these facility types are provided in the Glossary of terms (Appendix B).

MENTAL HOSPITALS
Mental hospitals are specialized hospital-based facilities that provide inpatient care and long-stay residential services for people with mental disorders. Usually these facilities are independent and stand alone, although they may have some links with the rest of the health-care system. In many countries, they remain the main type of mental health care facility. **Table 4.1.1** provides a summary of mental hospital indicators by WHO region and World Bank country income group. Based on reported data, there are 6.5 mental hospital beds per 100,000 population.

Despite the transition in a number of high-income countries towards psychiatric wards in general hospitals and the provision of community-based residential care places, high-income countries still have a far higher number of mental hospital beds (41.8 per 100,000 population) and admission rates (142.3 per 100,000 population) than lower-income countries. Analyzed by WHO region, there are 35 beds per 100,000 population in the European Region compared to less than ten in all other Regions; similarly, admission rates in the European Region exceed 200 per 100,000 population, compared to less than 50 elsewhere. Levels of follow-up for discharged mental hospital inpatients is reported to be 73% overall, but with notably lower rates reported for the Region of the Americas (34%) and the Eastern Mediterranean Region (55%).

	Facilities (total population per facility, in millions) (N = 153)	**Beds** (rate per 100,000 population) (N = 141)	**Admissions** (rates per 100,000 population) (N = 118)	**Continuity** (% discharged patients seen within a month) (N = 26)
Global	2.85	6.5	35.8	73%
WHO region				
AFRO	8.36	1.9	10.5	84%
AMRO	1.34	8.7	44.2	34%
EMRO	4.15	4.2	27.9	55%
EURO	0.64	35.0	238.6	81%
SEARO	28.78	2.1	14.5	89%
WPRO	7.48	3.5	2.8	79%
Income group				
Low-income	11.67	1.6	7.6	47%
Lower-middle income	4.40	4.0	14.4	80%
Upper-middle income	1.78	14.4	41.9	63%
High-income	0.78	41.8	142.3	76%

TABLE 4.1.1 Mental hospital indicators by WHO region and World Bank country income group

RESULTS
MENTAL HEALTH SERVICE AVAILABILITY AND UPTAKE

A further question asked of countries relates to the duration of stay in mental hospitals, results for which are shown in **Figures 4.1.1-4.1.2** (for the 41 countries providing data). This shows that in most regions of the world, the great majority of inpatients are discharged within one year (global median, 80%). However, in certain regions including the American, Eastern Mediterranean and Western Pacific Regions, there is still a significant proportion (40% or more) of mental hospital residents who have had a length of stay of more than one year or even five years. The particularly high value for the Region of the Americas reflects the fact that a large proportion of countries responding to this item were from the Caribbean, a number of which reported these high rates.

PSYCHIATRIC WARDS

Psychiatric wards in general hospitals are psychiatric units that provides inpatient care within a community-based hospital facility (e.g. general hospital). These units provide care to users with acute psychiatric problems, and the period of stay is usually relatively short (weeks to months). **Table 4.1.2** provides a summary of indicators for psychiatric wards in general hospitals by WHO region and World Bank country income group. Globally, there are 2.1 beds per 100,000 population (three times less than mental hospital beds), but this masks substantial differences between regions and country income groups; for example, there are over 10 beds per 100,000 population in high-income countries compared to less than 1 in low-income and lower-middle income countries. Similar differences are seen for the rate of admissions and the number of facilities. Again, the European Region has a far higher rate of facilities, beds and admissions than other Regions. In order to assess continuity of care – a marker for the quality of the mental health care system – Atlas 2014 also enquired about the proportion of inpatients discharged from these units who had been followed-up within one month. Reported rates on this indicator (from only a small number of countries) were generally high, with a global median of 87% (which is higher than the global rate of 73% reported for mental hospitals); this implies better levels of coordination with community-based services. Similarly, the admission rate for psychiatric wards in general hospitals is higher than that for mental hospitals, which indicates average stays and more efficient use of hospital resources.

	Facilities (total population per facility, in millions) (N = 139)	Beds (rate per 100,000 population) (N = 126)	Admissions (rates per 100,000 population) (N = 89)	Continuity (% discharged patients seen within a month) (N = 22)
Global	1.22	2.1	43.8	87%
WHO region				
AFRO	3.65	0.7	10.1	96%
AMRO	1.31	0.8	58.0	94%
EMRO	4.31	0.5	13.8	74%
EURO	0.35	10.8	131.8	59%
SEARO	2.76	0.6	32.9	85%
WPRO	0.25	2.2	74.9	90%
Income group				
Low-income	4.15	0.5	3.8	90%
Lower-middle income	3.19	0.6	7.8	90%
Upper-middle income	1.14	2.8	58.6	80%
High-income	0.29	11.5	126.8	85%

TABLE 4.1.2 Summary of indicators for psychiatric wards in general hospitals, by WHO region and World Bank country income group

MENTAL HEALTH ATLAS 2014

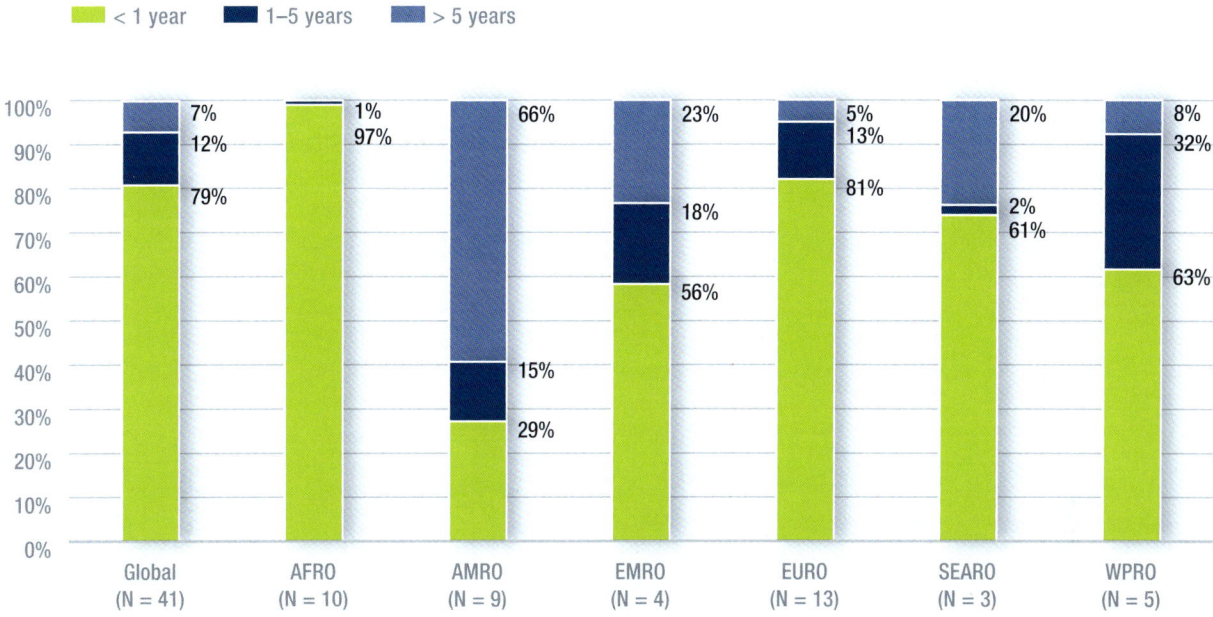

FIG. 4.1.1 Duration of stay in mental hospitals, by WHO region
(median percentage values)

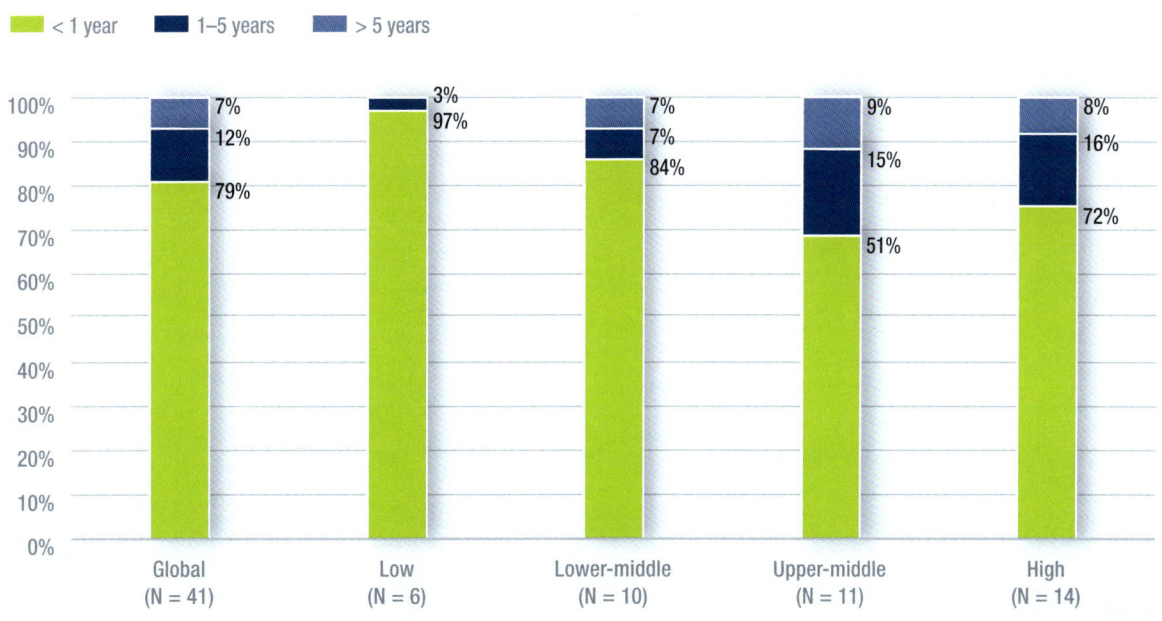

FIG. 4.1.2 Duration of stay in mental hospitals, by World Bank income level
(median percentage values)

RESULTS | MENTAL HEALTH SERVICE AVAILABILITY AND UPTAKE

RESULTS
MENTAL HEALTH SERVICE AVAILABILITY AND UPTAKE

COMMUNITY-BASED RESIDENTIAL CARE FACILITIES

Community-based residential care facilities, which typically serve users with relatively stable and chronic mental disorders, are an almost non-existent resource in low- and middle-income countries (according to submitted Atlas data from 85 countries). In high-income countries, by comparison, there are 10 residential care beds per 100,000 population, thereby identifying them as an important resource in the overall provision of mental health care services.

Based on the data presented in Tables 4.1.1 and 4.1.2, **Figures 4.1.3-4.1.4** show the overall number of beds per 100,000 population, by WHO Region and World Bank income group respectively.

INVOLUNTARY ADMISSIONS

79 countries provided data about the proportion of inpatient admissions to mental hospitals, psychiatric wards in general hospitals and community residential facilities that are involuntary. Across all facility types, more than one in ten (11.6%) of admissions globally were on an involuntary basis. For mental hospitals more specifically, the global rate is higher (17%, based on 56 responses) and in some Regions reaches more than 60% (South East Asia and Western Pacific Regions).

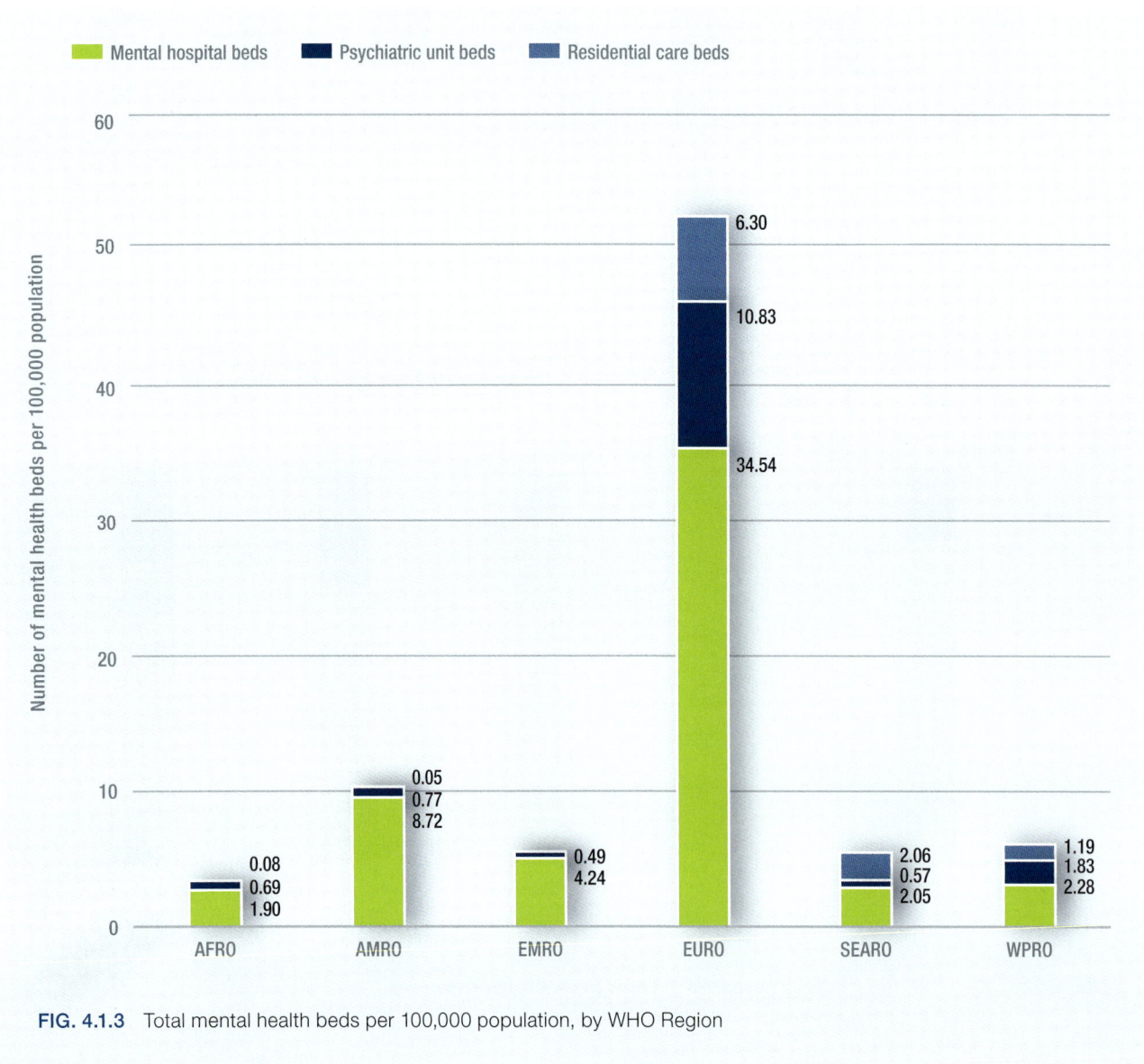

FIG. 4.1.3   Total mental health beds per 100,000 population, by WHO Region

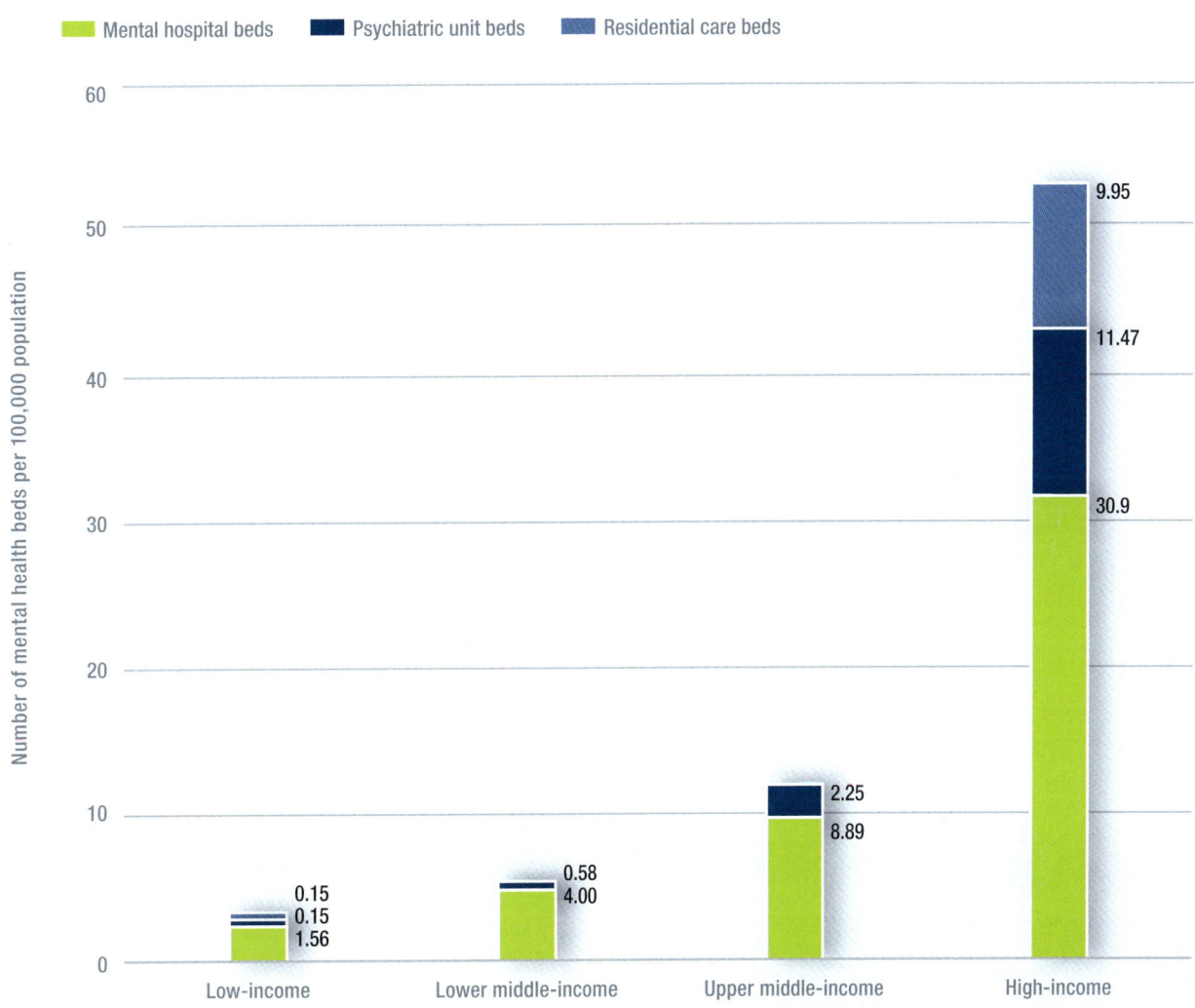

FIG. 4.1.4 Total mental health beds per 100,000 population, by World Bank income group

RESULTS
MENTAL HEALTH SERVICE AVAILABILITY AND UPTAKE

4.2 OUTPATIENT CARE

Outpatient care is composed of hospital outpatient departments, mental health outpatient clinics, community mental health centres, and community-based mental health care facilities, including day-care centres. Definitions for these types of facilities are provided in Appendix B. Similar to the findings for residential care as a mode of inpatient care, day care facilities are essentially absent in the context of low- and middle-income countries. In high-income countries, the median value for 18 responding countries was 5.3 places per 100,000 population.

Mental health outpatient facilities manage mental disorders and related clinical and social problems on an outpatient basis. As shown in **Table 4.2.1**, the availability and utilisation of outpatient facilities is dramatically different for countries of different income levels: the number of visits per 100,000 population in high-income countries (6,668) is over 50 times greater than in low-income countries (102) and 20 times greater than lower-middle income countries (320). Similar disparities are seen between Regions, with the African Region in particular having an extremely low rate of visits per 100,000 population.

Expressing these outpatient visits as a percentage of all inpatient admissions and outpatient visits reveals that across all country income groups and in most WHO regions at least 90% of total service contacts are through outpatient services; in the African Region, however, the proportion is considerably less (41%).

	Facilities (total population per facility, in millions) (N = 89)	Visits (rate per 100,000 population) (N = 89)
Global	0.17	1,051
WHO region		
AFRO	3.31	14
AMRO	0.07	1,165
EMRO	1.02	990
EURO	0.08	6,688
SEARO	0.14	320
WPRO	0.06	2,321
Income group		
Low-income	3.08	102
Lower-middle income	0.37	320
Upper-middle income	0.11	1,574
High-income	0.05	6,688

TABLE 4.2.1 Summary of outpatient care facilities indicators by WHO region and World Bank country income group (median)

4.3 TREATED PREVALENCE

Treated prevalence refers to the proportion of people with mental disorders served by mental health systems. The number of people per 100,000 population who received care for mental disorders in the various types of mental health facilities (outpatient facilities, day care facilities, psychiatric wards in general hospitals and mental hospitals) over the previous year can serve as a proxy for treated prevalence in specialist mental health care services (**Figure 4.3.1**). Reflecting service availability indicators, the derived level of treated prevalence in low-income countries is both absolutely and – when compared to high-income countries – relatively low.

Data were also requested for cases treated in primary health care and social care service settings, but the response rate to these items was extremely limited and too low to use for global reporting or regional comparisons. Such limitations in the availability of data makes it unfeasible to determine overall treatment coverage in the population.

4.4 SOCIAL SUPPORT

As shown in **Figure 4.4.1**, the rate of persons with severe mental disorder who receive disability payments, income support or other forms of non-monetary support (e.g. housing support, access to employment) is strongly influenced by income level, with a far higher rate of support seen in high-income countries (520 persons per 100,000 population) compared to lower-income countries (12-14 in low and lower-middle income countries, and 73 in upper-middle income countries). However, this item suffered from a low response rate, and there was insufficient data to provide a breakdown, either by severity of mental disorder or by type of support (monetary versus non-monetary).

MENTAL HEALTH ATLAS 2014

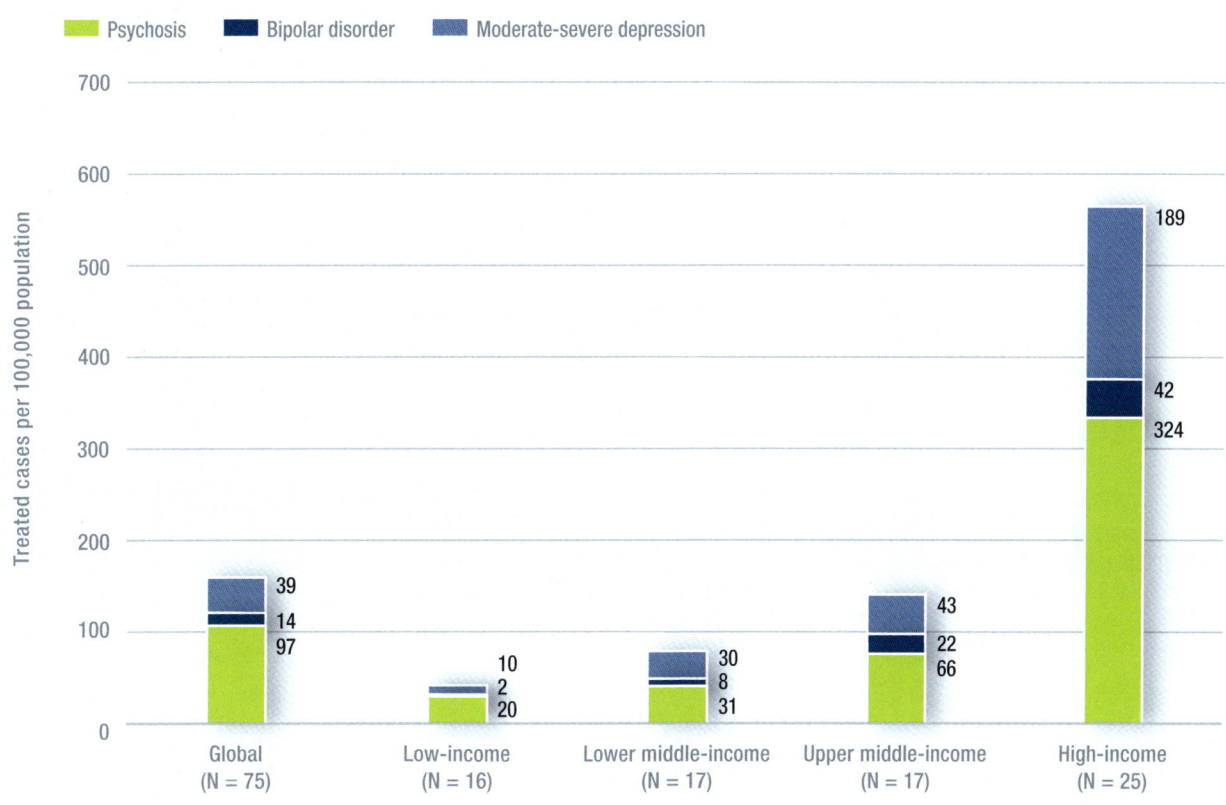

FIG. 4.3.1 Treated prevalence of severe mental disorders per 100,000 population in specialist mental health services

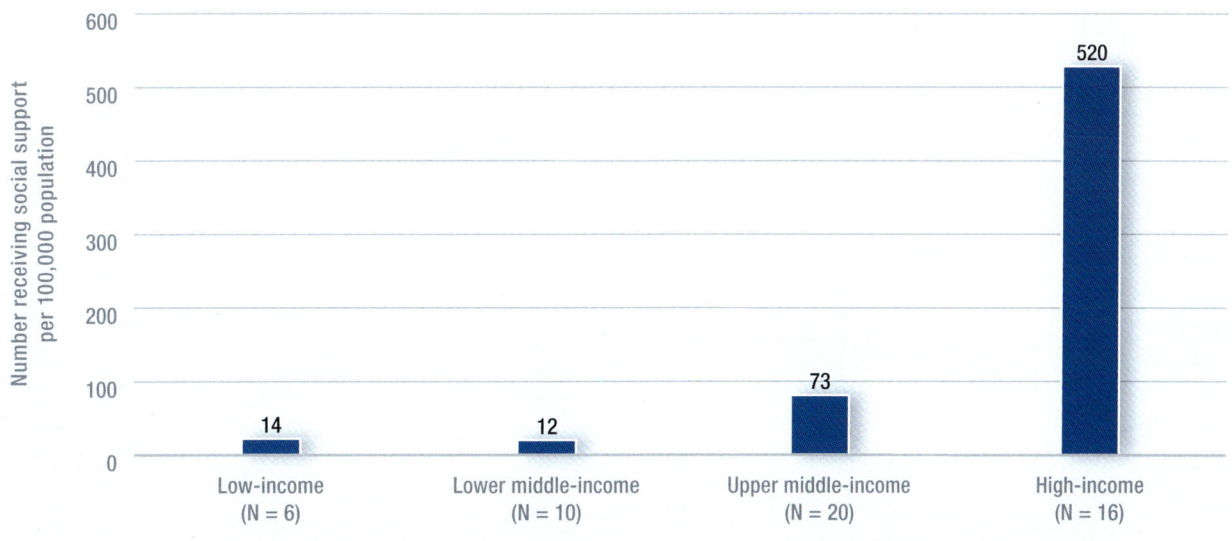

FIG. 4.4.1 Social support for persons with severe mental disorders

RESULTS

5. MENTAL HEALTH PROMOTION AND PREVENTION

5.1 MENTAL HEALTH PROMOTION AND PREVENTION PROGRAMMES

In the context of national efforts to develop and implement mental health policies and programmes, it is vital to meet not only the needs of persons with defined mental disorders, but also to protect and promote the mental well-being of all citizens. Accordingly, Objective 3 of the Mental Health Action Plan concerns the implementation of strategies for promotion and prevention in mental health, including prevention of suicide and self-harm. Global Target 3.1 is for 80% of countries to have at least two functioning national, multisectoral promotion and prevention programmes in mental health (by the year 2020). Examples of broad strategies for mental health promotion and the prevention of mental disorders across the life course include information campaigns; promotion of the rights; early childhood and life skills programmes; provision of healthy working conditions; and protection programmes that tackle child abuse as well as other violence at domestic and community levels.

Mental health Atlas 2014 has identified ongoing prevention and promotion efforts at the country level. To be considered 'functional', a programme needed to have at least two of the following three characteristics: a) dedicated financial and human resources; b) a defined plan of implementation; and c) evidence of progress and/or impact. Programmes which did not meet this threshold, or which were evidently related to treatment or care, were excluded.

In total, 80 out of 194 WHO Member States (41%) have at least two functioning mental health promotion and prevention programmes, close to half the 2020 Global Target of 80%. Achievement rates are similar across WHO regions (**Figure 5.1.1**). Many countries have more than two functioning programmes, especially in the European Region; a total of 411 were identified through the ATLAS questionnaire (**Figure 5.1.2**).

Over and above their regional distribution, programmes were categorised according to their geographical scope (national, regional, district), their ownership/management (government, NGO, private), the type of programme (universal, selective or indicated prevention), as well as the primary target or purpose of the programme (in terms of disorder/condition, age group and population group). Findings are displayed in **Figures 5.1.3-5.1.4**.

In terms of the overall type of programme, close to half could be described as universal prevention (interventions targeted at the general public or to a whole population group) (**Figure 5.1.3**) while a further quarter are related to selective prevention (which targets individuals or subgroups of the population with an elevated risk of developing a mental disorder). 12% involved targeted or indicated prevention for high-risk people identified as having detectable signs or symptoms indicating mental disorder. The high proportion of universal prevention programmes is reflected in the breakdown by age group (50% of programmes are targeted at all ages).

Looking across the types of programme reported on, over half (55%) could be described as mental health awareness programmes aimed at improving mental health literacy or combating stigma and discrimination, either in the form of specific events or through multimedia (**Figure 5.1.4**). The next most common type of programme were school-based promotion interventions (11%) and workplace initiatives (9%).

RESULTS
MENTAL HEALTH PROMOTION AND PREVENTION

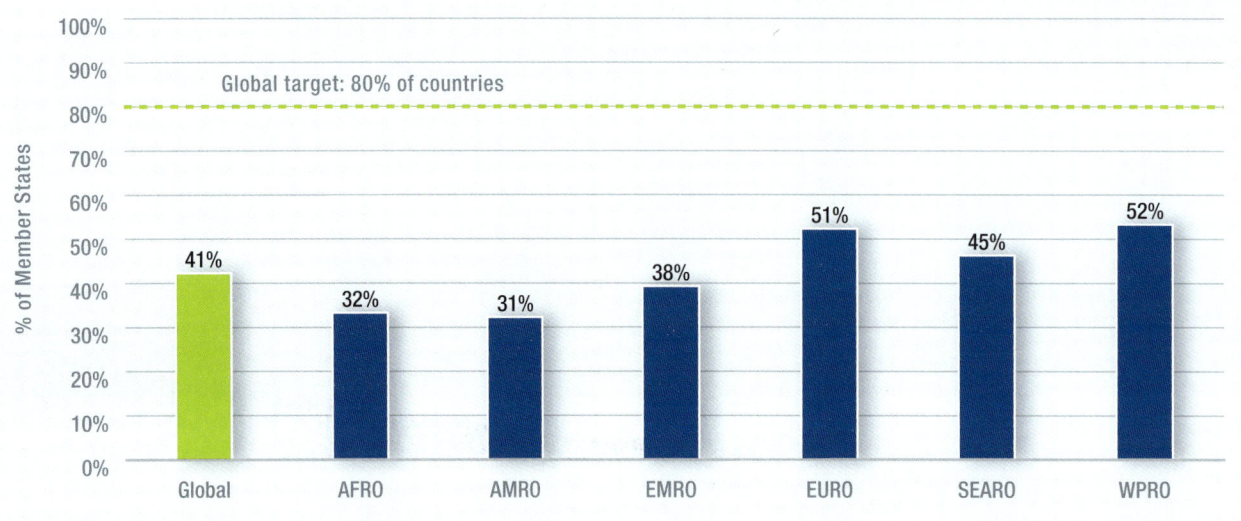

FIG. 5.1.1 Promotion and prevention programmes: Proportion of countries with at least two functioning programmes

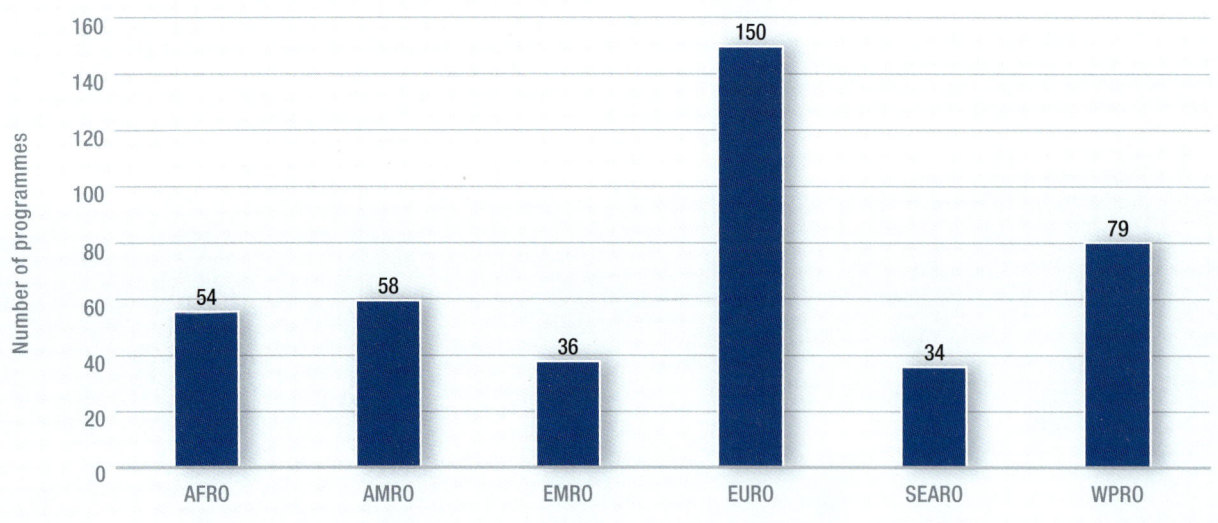

FIG. 5.1.2 Promotion and prevention programmes (N = 411): Regional breakdown

MENTAL HEALTH ATLAS 2014

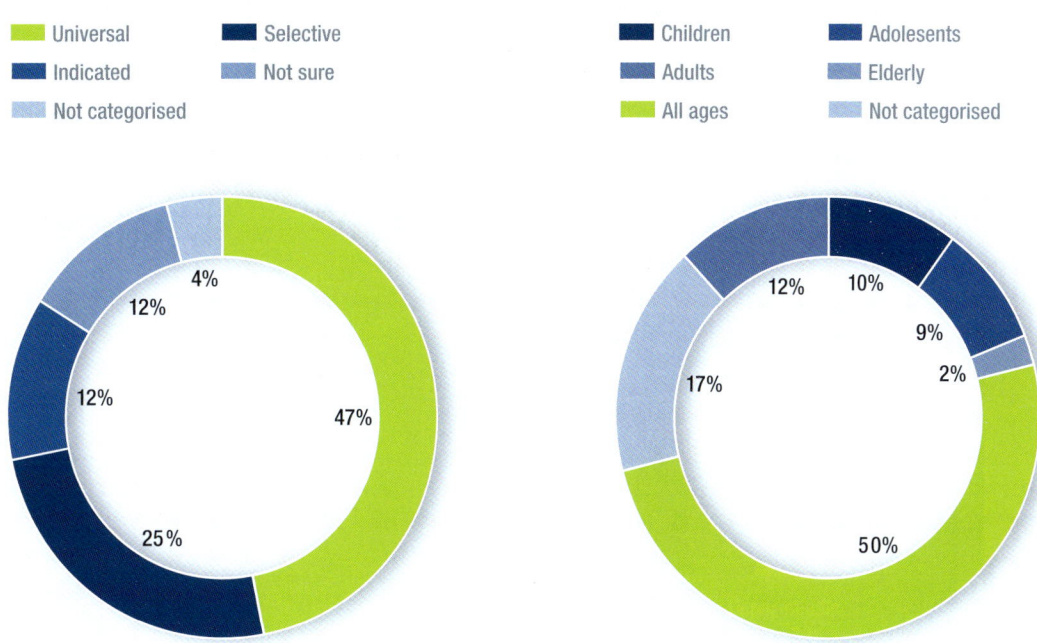

FIG. 5.1.3 Promotion and prevention programmes: Form of prevention and age group

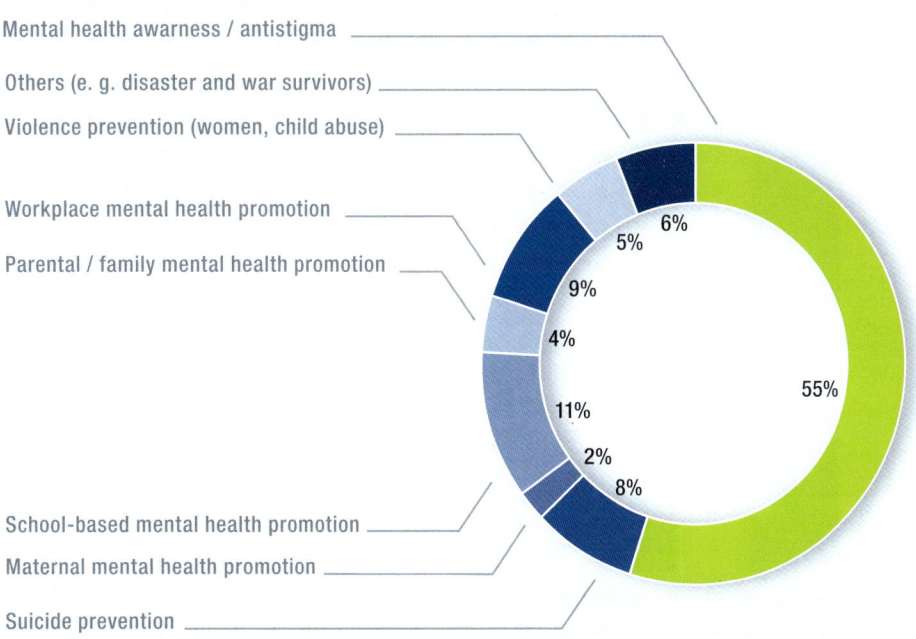

FIG. 5.1.4 Promotion and prevention programmes (N = 411): Main types of programme

RESULTS
MENTAL HEALTH PROMOTION AND PREVENTION

5.2 SUICIDE PREVENTION

A particular prevention priority in the area of mental health concerns suicide, which accounted for an estimated 804,000 deaths in 2012 (WHO, 2014). Target 3.2 of the Mental Health Action Plan calls for a 10% reduction in the rate of suicide by 2020.

Given weak vital registration systems in many countries, and known problems of under-reporting suicide as a cause of death, the most consistent and reliable estimates for rates of suicide in different regions of the world comes from the recent WHO global report on suicide (WHO, 2014). The global, age-standardized rate of suicide in 2012 was estimated to be 11.4 per 100,000 population; this provides the best available baseline value for 2013 against which to measure progress towards reducing the suicide rate over the period of the Mental Health Action Plan.

Figure 5.2.1 provides age-standardized suicide rates in different regions of the world. Rates are higher among males than females, reaching 20 per 100,000 population in high-income countries and also in lower-income countries of Europe and South-East Asia.

Atlas 2014 did also request data on number of suicide deaths (by age and sex), with a view to increasing the amount of nationally sourced information, and these data will be used to improve national-level suicide rate estimates.

Atlas 2014 also asked countries to report whether they had a national suicide prevention strategy. Results show that currently no low-income and less than 10% of lower-middle income countries have developed such a strategy, while close to one-third of upper-middle and high-income countries report having developed such a strategy.

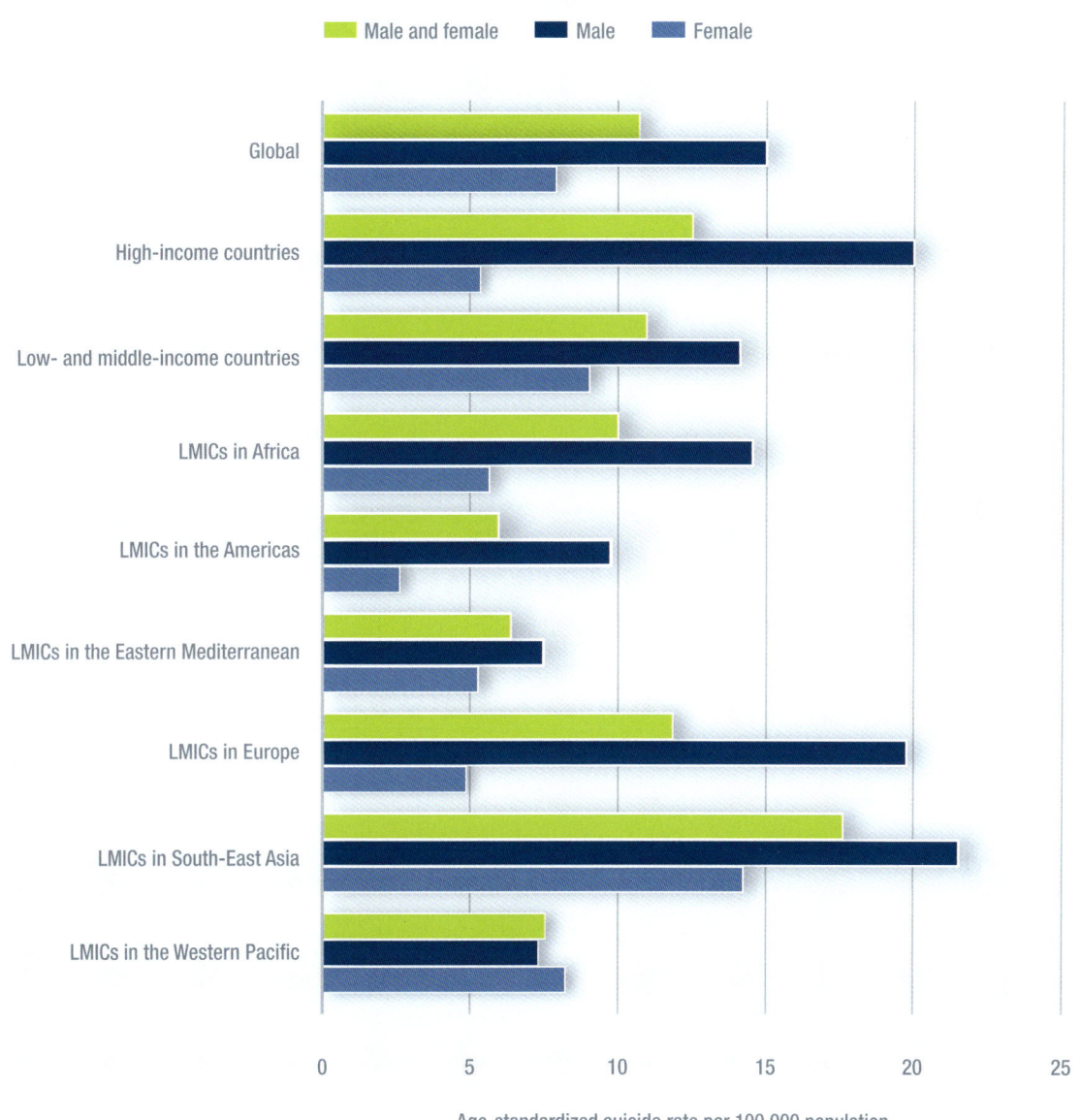

FIG. 5.2.1 Age-standardized suicide rate in different regions of the world, 2012

Source: WHO (2014)   Note: LMICs = Low and middle-income countries

RESULTS

6. COMPARISONS WITH ATLAS 2011 RESULTS

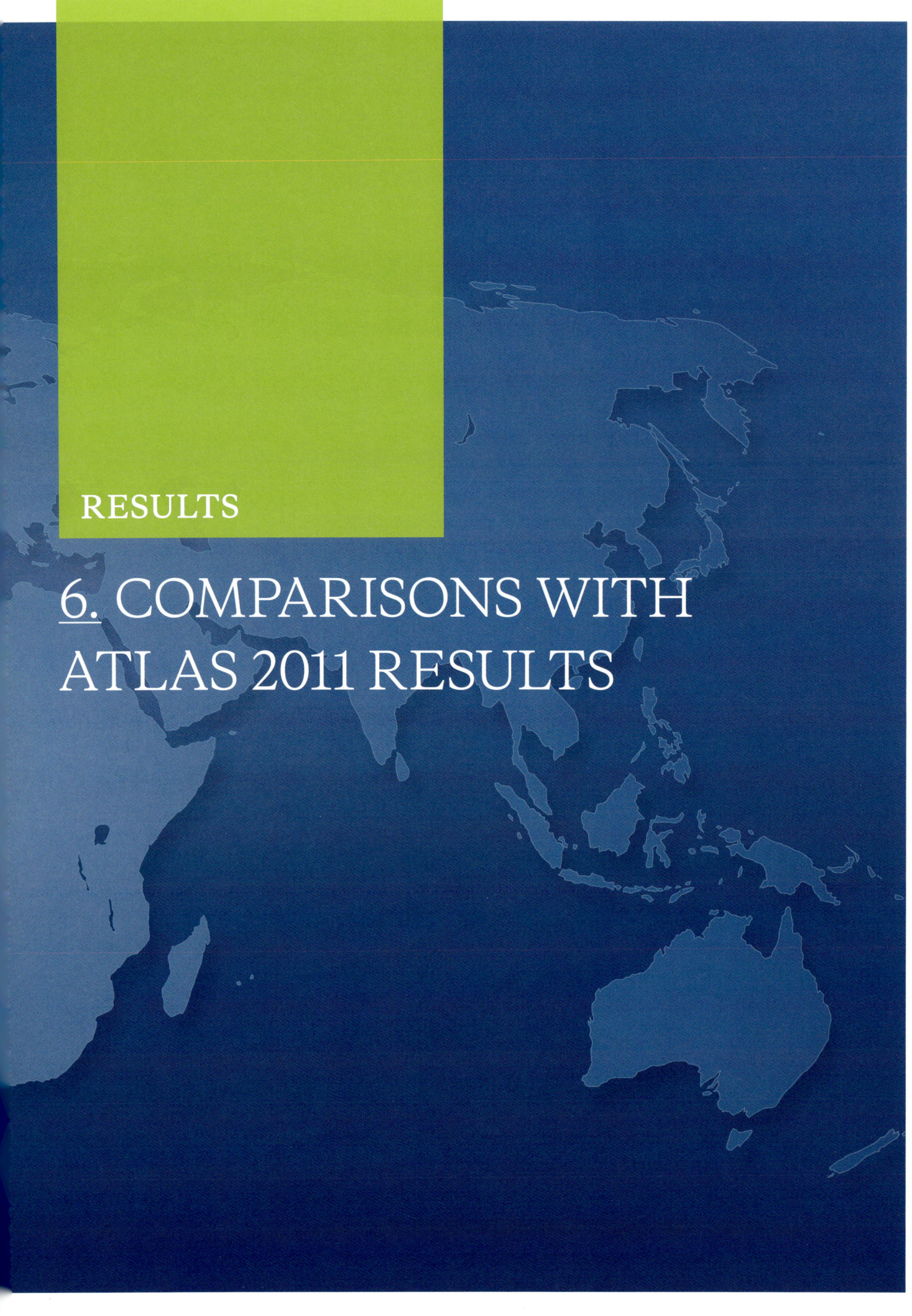

Utilisation of Atlas datasets at successive time points can provide important information and insights into emerging trends with respect to mental health policies, laws, services and resources. However, such comparisons of data over time are heavily constrained by the requirement to have country data available at all relevant time points. Reporting changes in global or regional values based on differing country datasets is methodologically flawed; accordingly, the country datasets used below include only those countries reporting data for the variable of interest both in 2011 and 2014. This revision to the underlying dataset used to generate global and regional estimates means that the median values below are expected to differ to some degree from the median values shown for the same variables reported in other sections of Atlas 2014 and 2011 reports. Comparisons were possible for a number of Atlas items only and are given below.

MENTAL HEALTH WORKFORCE

There has been a slight decline (of 6%) in the reported number of psychiatrists between 2011 and 2014 (**Table 6.1**). This finding may reflect under-reporting in the 2014 survey of psychiatrists working in private practice (particular emphasis had been given to this in the 2011 survey). In the South-East Asian and African Regions, the reported number of psychiatrists has increased by more than 25% (albeit from a very low baseline rate in 2011). The median of nurses working in mental health globally has shifted upwards by 37%, with particularly notable increases seen in the American Region (63%) and Eastern Mediterranean Regions (46%). The positive change in the number of nurses working in mental health is greatest in low-income countries and least in high-income countries. However, the absolute number of nurses working in mental health in high-income countries is still many times higher than in lower income country groups.

	Psychiatrists (median rate per 100,000 population)				Nurses (median rate per 100,000 population)			
	N	2014	2011	Change	N	2014	2011	Change
Global	118	0.93	0.99	–6%	106	5.31	3.89	37%
WHO region								
AFRO	32	0.07	0.05	34%	29	0.70	0.76	–8%
AMRO	24	1.09	1.08	1%	21	6.08	3.73	63%
EMRO	12	0.78	0.98	–21%	13	3.10	2.12	46%
EURO	28	7.43	7.65	–3%	21	22.07	21.93	1%
SEARO	7	0.36	0.28	27%	5	2.74	2.92	–6%
WPRO	15	0.91	0.90	1%	17	3.79	4.88	–22%
Income group								
Low	24	0.05	0.05	–2%	23	0.36	0.26	41%
Lower-middle	33	0.38	0.33	15%	30	2.73	2.26	20%
Upper-middle	34	1.39	1.61	–13%	32	8.20	7.09	16%
High	27	7.47	8.18	–8%	21	33.24	30.76	8%

TABLE 6.1 Change in number of psychiatrists and nurses working in mental health

RESULTS
COMPARISONS WITH ATLAS 2011 RESULTS

HOSPITAL BEDS AND ADMISSIONS

Globally, there was a slight decrease of 5% in the number of mental hospitals between 2011 and 2014. A more significant decrease is observed for the number of mental hospital beds, which has dropped by nearly 30% compared to 2011 (**Table 6.2**). In all WHO regions, there was a decline in the number of beds, particularly in the Region of the Americas (a 45% decrease). When countries were grouped according to income level, all except the lower middle-income category showed a reduction in both number of hospitals and number of mental hospital beds.

At the global level, the number of beds available in psychiatric wards in general hospital has shown a marked increase of 60% between 2011 and 2014. In the Western Pacific Region, for example, psychiatric beds in general hospitals increased by more than 8 times since 2011.

Despite the global decrease in number of beds, there was an increase of over 20% in the global median of admission rate to mental hospitals (**Table 6.3**), indicative of a higher turnover rate. The trends across WHO regions are mixed; for example, the Western Pacific Region shows a decline of more than 50%, while the Eastern Mediterranean and South-East Asian Regions show an increase of 25%. In high-income countries there was a 19% decrease in admission rates to mental hospitals while there was a slight increase (of 2%) in low-income countries.

Admission rates to general hospital facilities has also increased substantially over this period (by 84%). Reported increases are particularly marked for the American, South-East Asian and Western Pacific Regions. When aggregated by income group, it is apparent that these increases are largely occurring in middle-income countries; admission rates in low-income and high-income country groups have actually decreased.

	Mental Hospital Beds (median rate per 100,000 population)				General Hospital Beds (median rate per 100,000 population)			
	N	2014	2011	Change	N	2014	2011	Change
Global	130	6.68	9.29	–28%	107	2.25	1.41	60%
WHO region								
AFRO	27	2.45	2.88	–15%	22	0.69	0.82	–15%
AMRO	25	6.55	11.87	–45%	20	1.28	0.90	42%
EMRO	17	4.24	5.10	–17%	12	0.37	0.87	–58%
EURO	36	37.01	38.81	–5%	34	10.02	10.35	–3%
SEARO	8	2.33	1.97	18%	5	0.57	0.30	92%
WPRO	17	3.49	4.49	–22%	14	4.01	0.44	812%
Income group								
Low	21	1.48	1.77	–16%	18	0.47	0.74	–37%
Lower-middle	31	4.80	4.51	6%	25	0.92	0.54	69%
Upper-middle	42	8.29	14.83	–44%	30	2.77	2.16	28%
High	36	34.54	36.12	–4%	34	11.15	11.61	–4%

TABLE 6.2 Change in number of beds in mental hospital and psychiatric wards in general hospitals

	Mental Hospital Admission (median rate per 100,000 population)				General Hospital Admission (median rate per 100,000 population)			
	N	2014	2011	Change	N	2014	2011	Change
Global	94	41.15	33.75	22%	94	43.79	23.74	84%
WHO region								
AFRO	16	16.12	14.31	13%	11	10.07	7.39	36%
AMRO	16	44.42	44.12	1%	12	50.06	19.01	163%
EMRO	14	29.76	23.88	25%	8	15.89	12.93	23%
EURO	28	183.76	256.70	–28%	22	126.83	138.89	–9%
SEARO	7	3.49	2.77	26%	4	45.65	0.10	>1,000%
WPRO	13	2.84	6.15	–54%	6	86.44	72.25	20%
Income group								
Low	16	9.36	9.19	2%	10	3.62	4.57	–21%
Lower-middle	20	15.98	19.36	–17%	14	5.97	4.74	26%
Upper-middle	27	41.89	55.70	–25%	16	50.86	27.36	86%
High	31	128.32	159.11	–19%	23	121.89	164.98	–26%

TABLE 6.3 Change in admissions to mental hospital and psychiatric wards in general hospitals

REFERENCES

1. WHO (2001).
   Mental health resources in the world 2001. World Health Organization, Geneva.
   http://www.who.int/mental_health/publications/mh_atlas_2001/en/

2. WHO (2005).
   Mental health Atlas 2005. World Health Organization, Geneva.
   http://www.who.int/mental_health/evidence/mhatlas05/en/

3. WHO (2011).
   Mental health Atlas 2011. World Health Organization, Geneva.
   http://www.who.int/mental_health/publications/mental_health_atlas_2011/en/

4. WHO (2013).
   Mental Health Action Plan 2013-2020. World Health Organization, Geneva.
   http://www.who.int/mental_health/publications/action_plan/en/

5. WHO (2014).
   Preventing suicide: a global imperative. World Health Organization, Geneva.
   http://www.who.int/mental_health/suicide-prevention/world_report_2014/en/

REFERENCES

APPENDIX A
PARTICIPATING COUNTRIES AND CONTRIBUTORS

WHO Member States	WHO region	World Bank income category	Contributors to Atlas 2014
Afghanistan	EMR	Low income	Bashir Ahmad Sarwari; Khesraw Parwiz
Albania	EUR	Upper middle income	Emanuela Tollozhina
Algeria	AFR	Upper middle income	Chakali Mohamed; Mesbah Smain
Andorra	EUR	High income	
Angola	AFR	Upper middle income	
Antigua and Barbuda	AMR	High income	
Argentina	AMR	Upper middle income	Maria Matilde Massa
Armenia	EUR	Lower middle income	Armen Soghoyan
Australia	WPR	High income	Chris Bedford
Austria	EUR	High income	Magdalena Arrouas
Azerbaijan	EUR	Upper middle income	Fuad Ismayilov; Geray Geraybeyli
Bahamas (the)	AMR	High income	
Bahrain	EMR	High income	Sharifa Bucheeri; Mariam Al-Jalahma
Bangladesh	SEAR	Low income	Waziul Alam Chowdhury; Helal Uddin Ahmed
Barbados	AMR	High income	Wasim Worrell
Belarus	EUR	Upper middle income	Karatkevich Tatiana V.; Henchman Denis V.
Belgium	EUR	High income	Pol Gerits
Belize	AMR	Upper middle income	Eleanor Bennett
Benin	AFR	Low income	Josiane Ezin Houngbe
Bhutan	SEAR	Lower middle income	Tandin Dorji; Dorji Wangchuk
Bolivia (Plurinational State of)	AMR	Lower middle income	Juvenal Alejandro Aguilar Pacheco; Aurelio Cruz Uruchi
Bosnia and Herzegovina	EUR	Upper middle income	
Botswana	AFR	Upper middle income	Patrick Zibochwa
Brazil	AMR	Upper middle income	Cinthia Lociks de Araujo; Roberto Tykanori Kinoshita
Brunei Darussalam	WPR	High income	Asfar Afridi; Hilda Ho
Bulgaria	EUR	Upper middle income	Hristo Hinkov
Burkina Faso	AFR	Low income	Isaïe Medah
Burundi	AFR	Low income	Miburo Joselyne; Kamwenubusa Godefroid
Cabo Verde	AFR	Lower middle income	
Cambodia	WPR	Low income	Chhit Sophal
Cameroon	AFR	Lower middle income	
Canada	AMR	High income	Ryan Mccullough
Central African Republic (the)	AFR	Low income	Caleb Kette; Justin Ndoyo
Chad	AFR	Low income	
Chile	AMR	High income	Mauricio Gómez Chamorro; Pedro Cocco
China	WPR	Upper middle income	Ning Ma
Colombia	AMR	Upper middle income	María Inés Bohorquez; Elkin de Jesús Osorio
Comoros (the)	AFR	Low income	
Congo (the)	AFR	Lower middle income	Alain Mouanga
Cook Islands	WPR	Upper middle income	Rangiau Fariu; Elizabeth Iro
Costa Rica	AMR	Upper middle income	Virginia Rosabal Camarillo; Hugo Chacon Ramirez
Côte d'Ivoire	AFR	Lower middle income	Delafosse Roger Charles Joseph
Croatia	EUR	High income	Neven Henigsberg; Danica Kramarić
Cuba	AMR	Upper middle income	Carmen Borrego Calzadilla

APPENDICES
PARTICIPATING COUNTRIES AND CONTRIBUTORS

WHO Member States	WHO region	World Bank income category	Contributors to Atlas 2014
Cyprus	EUR	High income	Yiannis Kalakoutas; Irene Georghiou - Kyriacou
Czech Republic (the)	EUR	High income	Petr Winkler
Democratic People's Republic of Korea (the)	SEAR	Low income	
Democratic Republic of the Congo	AFR	Low income	Ildéphonse Muteba Mushidi;
Denmark	EUR	High income	Mille Pedersen
Djibouti	EMR	Lower middle income	Idd Wais Ibrahim
Dominica	AMR	Upper middle income	Griffin Benjamin; David Johnson
Dominican Republic (the)	AMR	Upper middle income	Jose Mieses Michel
Ecuador	AMR	Upper middle income	Aimée Dubois; Roberto Celi
Egypt	EMR	Lower middle income	Amina Mohamed Lotfy; Hisham Ramy
El Salvador	AMR	Lower middle income	Arturo Carranza Rivas; Julio Oscar Robles Ticas
Equatorial Guinea	AFR	High income	
Eritrea	AFR	Low income	Ghideon Yirgaw; Andeberhan Tesfazion
Estonia	EUR	High income	Andrea Kink; Ingrid Ots-Vaik
Ethiopia	AFR	Low income	Abdissa Kurkie
Fiji	WPR	Upper middle income	Jane Andrews, Eloni Tora
Finland	EUR	High income	Helena Vorma
France	EUR	High income	Philippe Leborgne
Gabon	AFR	Upper middle income	
Gambia (the)	AFR	Low income	Bakary Sonko
Georgia	EUR	Lower middle income	Sofio Morgoshia
Germany	EUR	High income	Stracke
Ghana	AFR	Lower middle income	Akwasi Osei
Greece	EUR	High income	Pavlos N. Theodorakis; Dimitra Siakotou
Grenada	AMR	Upper middle income	Joanna Humphrey; Myrna Hagley
Guatemala	AMR	Lower middle income	Licda. Susana Lemus; Ana Castellanos
Guinea	AFR	Low income	
Guinea-Bissau	AFR	Low income	
Guyana	AMR	Lower middle income	Bhiro Persaud Harry
Haiti	AMR	Low income	John Justafort
Honduras	AMR	Lower middle income	Carolina Padilla; Silvia Nazar
Hungary	EUR	Upper middle income	Tamás Kurimay
Iceland	EUR	High income	Guðrún Sigurjónsdóttir; Sveinn Magnússon
India	SEAR	Lower middle income	Sujeet K. Singh
Indonesia	SEAR	Lower middle income	Siti Chadidjah Nurillah; Eka Viora
Iran (Islamic Republic of)	EMR	Upper middle income	Ahmad Hajebi
Iraq	EMR	Upper middle income	Emad Abdulrazaq Abdulghani
Ireland	EUR	High income	
Israel	EUR	High income	Daphna Levinson; Tal Bergman-Levi
Italy	EUR	High income	Teresa Di Fiandra
Jamaica	AMR	Upper middle income	Maureen Irons Morgan; Kevin Harvey
Japan	WPR	High income	Toshihiro Horiguchi; Ichiro Tomisawa
Jordan	EMR	Upper middle income	Basheer Al Qaseer

WHO Member States	WHO region	World Bank income category	Contributors to Atlas 2014
Kazakhstan	EUR	Upper middle income	
Kenya	AFR	Low income	David M. Kiima
Kiribati	WPR	Lower middle income	Mireta Noere
Kuwait	EMR	High income	Adel Ahmed Alzayed
Kyrgyzstan	EUR	Lower middle income	Musabaeva Sabira
Lao People's Democratic Republic (the)	WPR	Lower middle income	Manivone Thikeo
Latvia	EUR	High income	Toms Pulmanis
Lebanon	EMR	Upper middle income	Wissam Kheir; Rabih El-chammai
Lesotho	AFR	Lower middle income	Michael Lebina
Liberia	AFR	Low income	Angie Tarr-Nyakoon; Tolbert G. Nyenswah
Libya	EMR	Upper middle income	
Lithuania	EUR	High income	Rolanda Adliene
Luxembourg	EUR	High income	Juliana D'Alimonte
Madagascar	AFR	Low income	Raharinivo
Malawi	AFR	Low income	Michael Udedi
Malaysia	WPR	Upper middle income	Nurashikin Ibrahim; Chong Chee Kheong
Maldives	SEAR	Upper middle income	Shanooha Mansoor
Mali	AFR	Low income	Baba Koumare
Malta	EUR	High income	Ray Xerri
Marshall Islands (the)	WPR	Upper middle income	Adri J. Hicking; Julia M. Alfred
Mauritania	AFR	Lower middle income	
Mauritius	AFR	Upper middle income	V. Ancharaz
Mexico	AMR	Upper middle income	Karla Maria Barragan Peña
Micronesia (Federated States of)	WPR	Lower middle income	
Monaco	EUR	High income	Dominique de Furst
Mongolia	WPR	Lower middle income	
Montenegro	EUR	Upper middle income	Zorica Barac-Otasevic
Morocco	EMR	Lower middle income	Zaki Hanane; Maaroufi Abderrahmane
Mozambique	AFR	Low income	Maria Lídia Gouveia
Myanmar	SEAR	Low income	Win Aung Myint
Namibia	AFR	Upper middle income	Albertina Barandonga
Nauru	WPR	Upper middle income	Samu Korovou
Nepal	SEAR	Low income	Surendra Sherchan
Netherlands (the)	EUR	High income	
New Zealand	WPR	High income	Barry Welsh; John Crawshaw
Nicaragua	AMR	Lower middle income	
Niger (the)	AFR	Low income	Yamien Ibrahim; Gado Habi
Nigeria	AFR	Lower middle income	Benard Ayaka Bene; Anthony Usoro
Niue	WPR	Upper middle income	
Norway	EUR	High income	Freja Ulvestad Kärki
Oman	EMR	High income	Hashim Zainy; Ahmed Al Busaidi
Pakistan	EMR	Lower middle income	Aahmood Ali; Fareed A. Minhas
Palau	WPR	Upper middle income	
Panama	AMR	Upper middle income	Ricardo Goti; Aldacira de Bradshaw; Itza Barahona de Mosca

APPENDICES
PARTICIPATING COUNTRIES AND CONTRIBUTORS

WHO Member States	WHO region	World Bank income category	Contributors to Atlas 2014
Papua New Guinea	WPR	Lower middle income	Umadevi Ambihaipahar
Paraguay	AMR	Lower middle income	Mirta Mendoza Bassani; Lida Sosa
Peru	AMR	Upper middle income	Yuri Cutipé Cardenas; Yuri Cutipé Cardenas
Philippines (the)	WPR	Lower middle income	Florante Trinidad
Poland	EUR	High income	Boguslaw Habrat; Dariusz Poznanski
Portugal	EUR	High income	Pedro Mateus; Miguel Xavier; Álvaro de Carvalho
Qatar	EMR	High income	Terry Sharkey; Salih Ali Al Marri
Republic of Korea (the)	WPR	High income	Yoon-Young Nam
Republic of Moldova (the)	EUR	Lower middle income	Jana Chihai
Romania	EUR	Upper middle income	Raluca Nica; Ileana Botezat Antonescu
Russian Federation (the)	EUR	High income	Kekelidze Zurab
Rwanda	AFR	Low income	Yvonne Kayiteshonga; Agnes Binagwaho
Saint Kitts and Nevis	AMR	High income	
Saint Lucia	AMR	Upper middle income	Naomi Jn Baptiste
Saint Vincent and the Grenadines	AMR	Upper middle income	Kerry-Ann Hamilton
Samoa	WPR	Lower middle income	Sina Georgina Fa'aiuga; George Tuitama; Leausa Toleafoa; Take Naseri; Leota Laki Lamositele Sio
San Marino	EUR	High income	Sebastiano Bastianelli
Sao Tome and Principe	AFR	Lower middle income	Yonelma Marques Daio
Saudi Arabia	EMR	High income	Abdulhameed A. Al-Habeeb
Senegal	AFR	Lower middle income	Aida Sylla
Serbia	EUR	Upper middle income	Dusica Lecic Tosevski
Seychelles	AFR	Upper middle income	Gina Michel
Sierra Leone	AFR	Low income	Andrew T.Muana; Brima Kargbo
Singapore	WPR	High income	Ong Lay Tin
Slovakia	EUR	High income	
Slovenia	EUR	High income	Mojca Zvezdana Dernovsek; Nadja Cobal
Solomon Islands	WPR	Lower middle income	Paul Orotaloa
Somalia	EMR	Low income	Zeynab Ahmed Noor; Mohamed Abdi Farah
South Africa	AFR	Upper middle income	Sifiso Phakathi; Precious Matsoso
South Sudan	AFR	Lower middle income	Mohamedi Boy Sebit
Spain	EUR	High income	José Rodríguez Escobar
Sri Lanka	SEAR	Lower middle income	Rasanjalee Hettiarachchi
Sudan (the)	EMR	Lower middle income	Zeinat Sanhori
Suriname	AMR	Upper middle income	Maltie Mohan-Algoe; Marthelise Eersel
Swaziland	AFR	Lower middle income	Violet D. Mwanjali
Sweden	EUR	High income	Tina Isaksson
Switzerland	EUR	High income	Elvira Keller-Guglielmetti
Syrian Arab Republic (the)	EMR	Lower middle income	Ramadan Mahfouri
Tajikistan	EUR	Low income	Kunguratov Hurshed
Thailand	SEAR	Upper middle income	Phunnapa Kittirattanapaiboon; Burin Suraaroonsamrit; Jedsada Chokdamrongsuk
The former Yugoslav Republic of Macedonia	EUR	Upper middle income	Aleksandar Risteski; Antoni Novotni

WHO Member States	WHO region	World Bank income category	Contributors to Atlas 2014
Timor-Leste	SEAR	Lower middle income	Anabela Clemetina da Costa Guterres; Herculano Seixas dos Santo
Togo	AFR	Low income	Kolou Dassa
Tonga	WPR	Upper middle income	Siale Akauola; Mapa H Puloka
Trinidad and Tobago	AMR	High income	Trudy Harding-Rouse
Tunisia	EMR	Upper middle income	Ouenniche Saida; Med Adel Ben Mahmoud
Turkey	EUR	Upper middle income	Esra Alataş, Seda Usubütün, Banu Nesibe Demir
Turkmenistan	EUR	Upper middle income	Dr Benueb
Tuvalu	WPR	Upper middle income	Kaeva Lototele
Uganda	AFR	Low income	Sheila Ndyanabangi
Ukraine	EUR	Lower middle income	
United Arab Emirates (the)	EMR	High income	Saleha Khalifa Bin Thiban
United Kingdom of Great Britain and Northern Ireland (the)	EUR	High income	Penny Curtis, Jane Verity
United Republic of Tanzania (the)	AFR	Low income	Norman B. Sabuni; Ayoub Magimba
United States of America (the)	AMR	High income	Winnifred I. Mitchell
Uruguay	AMR	High income	Ariel Montalbán; Denisse Dogmanas; Fernanda Porteiro
Uzbekistan	EUR	Lower middle income	Kharabara Grigory
Vanuatu	WPR	Lower middle income	Rufina Latu; Jimmy Obed
Venezuela (Bolivarian Republic of)	AMR	Upper middle income	
Viet Nam	WPR	Lower middle income	La Duc Cuong; Tran Trung Ha
Yemen	EMR	Lower middle income	Mohmammed Al-Khulaidy
Zambia	AFR	Lower middle income	Friday Nsalamo; John Mayeya
Zimbabwe	AFR	Low income	Dorcas Shirley Sithole; Gerald Gwinji

Associate Members, Areas and Territories*	
Anguilla	Bonnie Richardson-Lake
Saint Martin	Sharmilla Muller, Virginia Asin
Tokelau	Tekie Timu Iosefa
West Bank and Gaza	Hazem Nayef Ashour

* Associate Members, Areas and Territories were not included in the WHO regional and World Bank income group analyses. However short descriptive profiles of each of these countries as well as all participating WHO Member States will be published in the WHO Mental Health and Substance Abuse website.

Note: *Although care has been taken to include names of all contributors, information on any omissions or inaccuracies can be communicated to WHO Secretariat at mhatlas@who.int*

APPENDIX B
GLOSSARY OF TERMS

TYPES OF FACILITY

Forensic inpatient unit:
An inpatient unit that is exclusively maintained for the evaluation or treatment of people with mental disorders who are involved with the criminal justice system. These units can be located in mental hospitals, general hospitals, or elsewhere.

Mental hospital:
A specialized hospital-based facility that provides inpatient care and long-stay residential services for people with mental disorders. Usually these facilities are independent and standalone, although they may have some links with the rest of the health care system. The level of specialization varies considerably: in some cases only long-stay custodial services are offered, in others specialized and short-term services are also available (rehabilitation services, specialist units for children and elderly, etc.)

- Includes: Both public and private non-profit and for-profit facilities; mental hospitals for children and adolescents only and mental hospitals for other specifics groups (e.g., elderly) are also included.

- Excludes: Community-based psychiatric inpatient units; forensic inpatient units and forensic hospitals. Facilities that treat only people with alcohol and substance abuse disorder or intellectual disability without an accompanying mental disorder diagnosis.

Psychiatric ward in a general hospital:
A psychiatric unit that provides inpatient care for the management of mental disorders within a community-based facility. These units are usually located within general hospitals, they provide care to users with acute problems, and the period of stay is usually short (weeks to months).

- Includes: Both public and private non-profit and for-profit facilities; psychiatric ward in general hospital; psychiatric unit in general hospital, community-based psychiatric inpatient units for children and adolescents only; community-based psychiatric inpatient units for other specific groups (e.g. elderly).

- Excludes: Mental hospitals; community residential facilities; facilities that treat only people with alcohol and substance abuse disorder or mental retardation.

Mental health community residential facility:
A non-hospital, community-based mental health facility that provides overnight residence for people with mental disorders. Usually these facilities serve users with relatively stable mental disorders not requiring intensive medical interventions.

- Includes: Supervised housing; un-staffed group homes; group homes with some residential or visiting staff; hostels with day staff; hostels with day and night staff; hostels and homes with 24-hour nursing staff; halfway houses; therapeutic communities. Both public and private nonprofit and for-profit facilities are included. Community residential facilities for children and adolescents only and community residential facilities for other specifics groups (e.g. elderly) are also included.

- Excludes: Facilities that treat only people with a diagnosis of alcohol and substance abuse disorder or intellectual disability; residential facilities in mental hospitals; generic facilities that are important for people with mental disorders, but that are not planned with their specific needs in mind (e.g. nursing homes and rest homes for elderly people, institutions treating neurological disorders, or physical disability problems).

Mental health day care facility:
A facility that typically provides care for users during the day. The facilities are generally: (1) available to groups of users at the same time (rather than delivering services to individuals one at a time), (2) expect users to stay at the facilities beyond the periods during which they have face-to-face contact with staff (i.e. the service is not simply based on users coming for appointments with staff and then leaving immediately after the appointment) and (3) involve attendances that last half or one full day.

- Includes: day centres; day care centres; sheltered workshops; club houses; drop-in centres; employment/rehabilitation workshops; social firms. Both public and private non-profit and for-profit facilities are included. Mental health day treatment facilities for children and adolescents only and mental health day treatment facilities for other specifics groups (e.g. elderly) are also included.

- Excludes: Facilities that treat only people with a diagnosis of alcohol and substance abuse disorder or intellectual disability without an accompanying mental disorder diagnosis; generic facilities that are important for people with mental disorders, but that are not planned with their specific needs in mind; day treatment facilities for inpatients are excluded.

APPENDICES
GLOSSARY OF TERMS

Mental health outpatient facility:
A facility that focuses on the management of mental disorders and the clinical and social problems related to it on an outpatient basis.

- Includes: Community mental health centres; mental health ambulatories; outpatient services for specific mental disorders or for specialized treatments; outpatient clinics located in mental hospitals or general hospitals ; mental health outpatient departments in general hospitals; mental health policlinics; specialized NGO clinics that have mental health staff and provide mental health outpatient care (e.g. for rape survivors or homeless people). Both public and private non-profit and for-profit facilities are included. Mental health outpatient facilities for children and adolescents only and mental health outpatient facilities for other specifics groups (e.g. elderly) are also included.

- Excludes: Private practice; facilities that treat only people with alcohol and substance abuse disorder or intellectual disability without an accompanying mental disorder diagnosis.

Other residential facility:
A residential facility that houses people with mental disorders but does not meet the definition for community residential facility or any other mental health facility defined for this instrument (community-based psychiatric inpatient unit, community residential facility, forensic inpatient unit, mental hospital).

- Includes: Residential facilities specifically for people with mental retardation, for people with substance abuse problems, or for people with dementia. Included are also residential facilities that formally are not mental health facilities but where, nevertheless, the majority of the people residing in the facilities have diagnosable mental disorders.

OTHER TERMS USED

Admissions:
The number of admissions in one year is the sum of all admissions to the facility within that year. This number is a duplicated count; in other words, if one user is admitted twice, it is counted as two admissions.

Mental health legislation:
Legal provisions related to mental health. These provisions typically focus on issues such as: civil and human rights protection of people with mental disorders, treatment facilities, personnel, professional training, and service structure.

Mental health plan:
A detailed scheme for implementing strategic actions that addresses the promotion of mental health, the prevention of mental disorders, and treatment and rehabilitation. Such a plan allows the implementation of the vision, values, principles and objectives defined in the policy.

Mental health policy:
Mental health policy is an organized set of values, principles and objectives for improving mental health and reducing the burden of mental disorders in a population. It defines a vision for future action.

Nurse:
A health professional having completed a formal training in nursing at a recognized, university-level school for a diploma or degree in nursing.

Occupational therapist:
A health professional having completed a formal training in occupational therapy at a recognized, university-level school for a diploma or degree in occupational therapy.

Other health or mental health worker:
A health or mental health worker that possesses some training in health care or mental health care but does not fit into any of the defined professional categories (e.g. medical doctors, nurses, psychologists, social workers, occupational therapists).

- Includes: Non-doctor/non-nurse primary care workers, professional and paraprofessional psychosocial counsellors, special mental health educators, and auxiliary staff.

- Excludes: This group does not include general staff for support services within health or mental health care settings (e.g. cooking, cleaning, security).

Patients treated in a mental hospital:
(a) the number of patients in the mental hospital at the beginning of the year plus (b) the number of admissions during the year.

Patients treated in a community residential facility:
(a) the number of users in the facility at the beginning of the year plus (b) the number of admissions to the facility during the year.

Patients treated through a mental health day treatment facility:
The number of users with at least one attendance for treatment at the facility within the year.

Patients treated in a mental health outpatient facility:
The number of users with at least one outpatient contact with the facility. A contact refers to a mental health intervention provided by a staff member of a mental health outpatient facility, whether the intervention occurs within the facility or elsewhere

Primary health care clinic:
A clinic that often offers the first point of entry into the health care system. Primary health care clinics usually provide the initial assessment and treatment for common health conditions and refer those requiring more specialized diagnosis and treatment to facilities with staff with a higher level of training.

Primary health care doctor:
A general practitioner, family doctor, or other non-specialized medical doctor working in a primary health care clinic.

Primary health care nurse:
A nurse working in a primary health care clinic.

Psychiatrist:
A medical doctor who has had at least two years of post-graduate training in psychiatry at a recognized teaching institution. This period may include training in any sub-specialty of psychiatry.

Psychologist:
A professional having completed a formal training in psychology at a recognized, university-level school for a diploma or degree in psychology.

Social worker:
A professional having completed a formal training in social work at a recognized, university-level school for a diploma or degree in social work.

User/Consumer/Patient:
A person receiving mental health care. These terms are used in different placesand by different groups of practitioners and people with mental disorders, and are used synonymously.